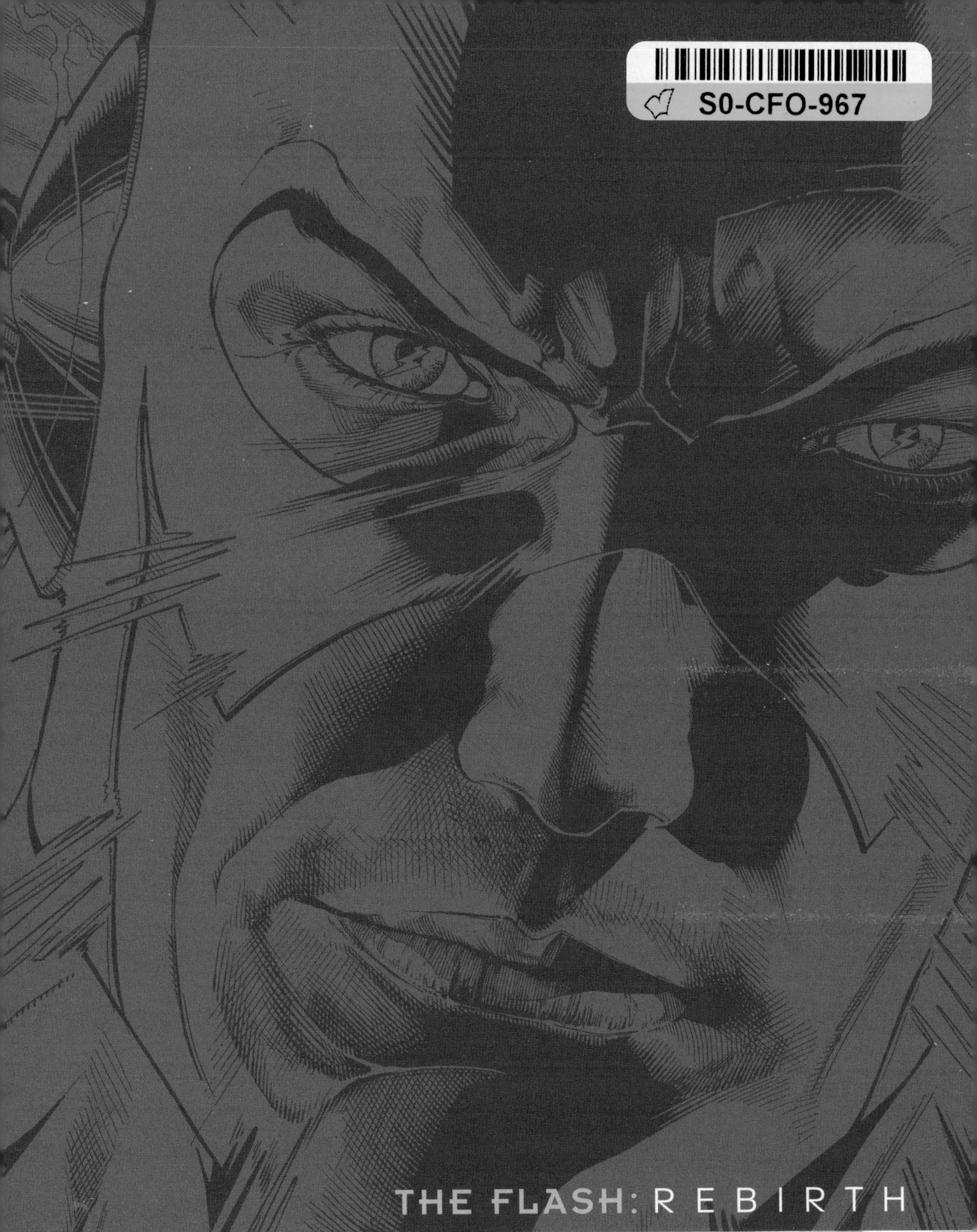
THE FLASH: REBIRTH

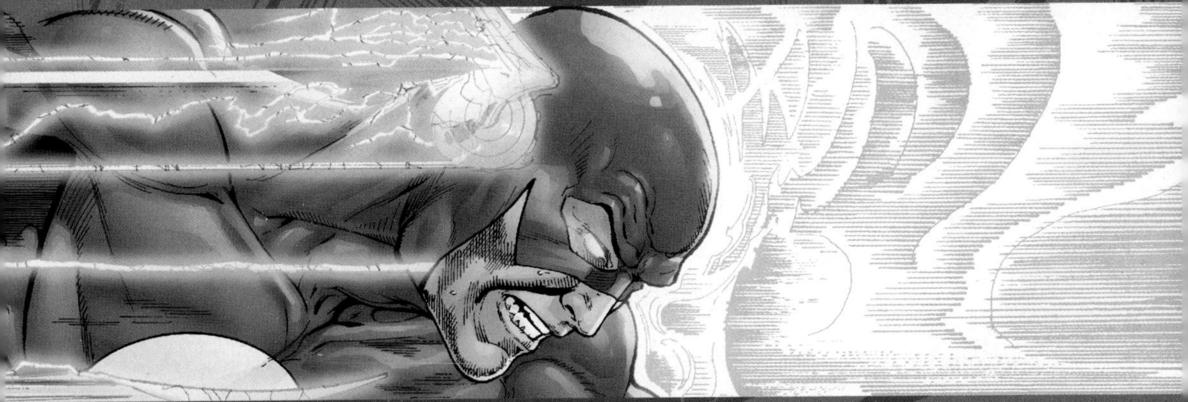

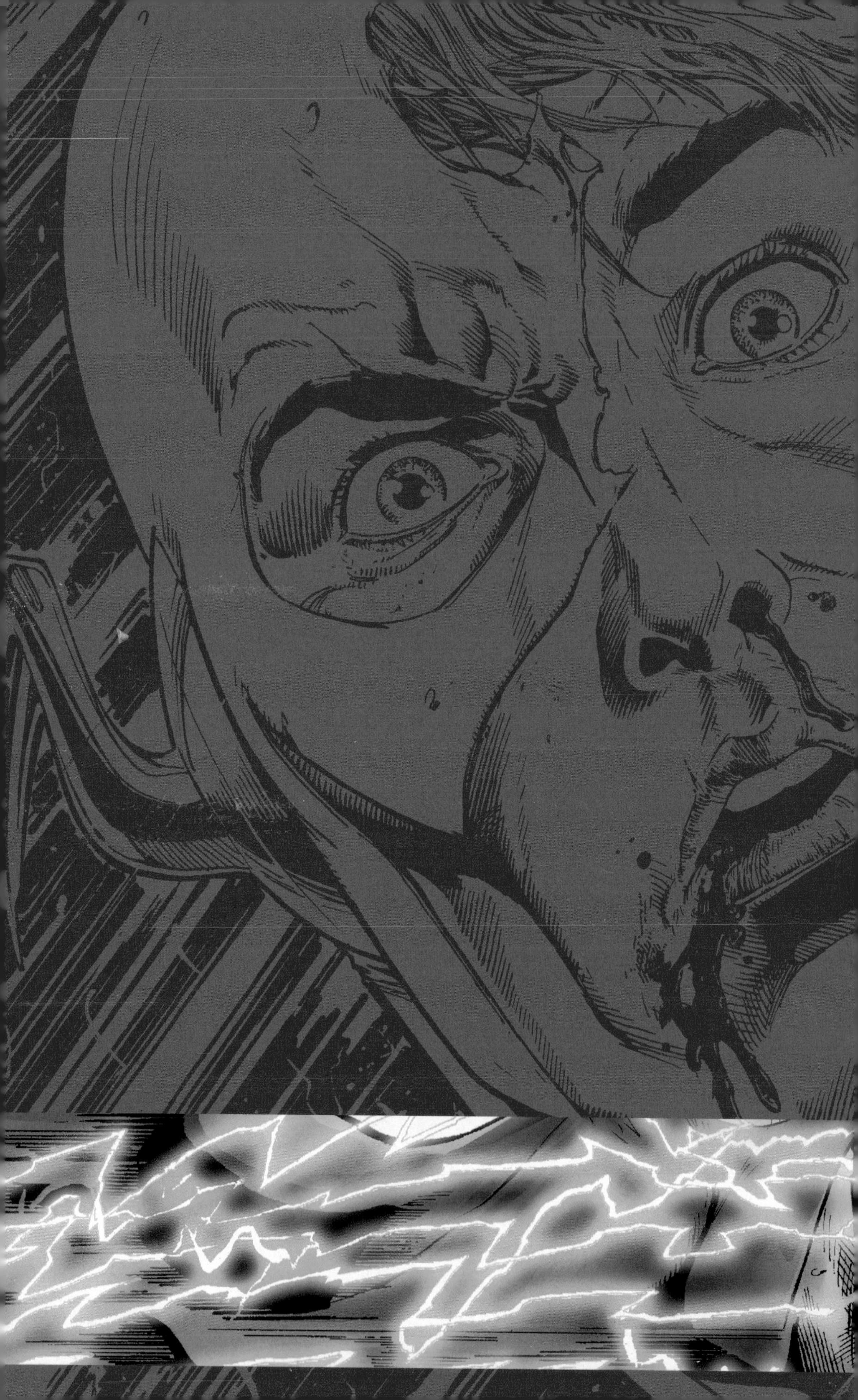

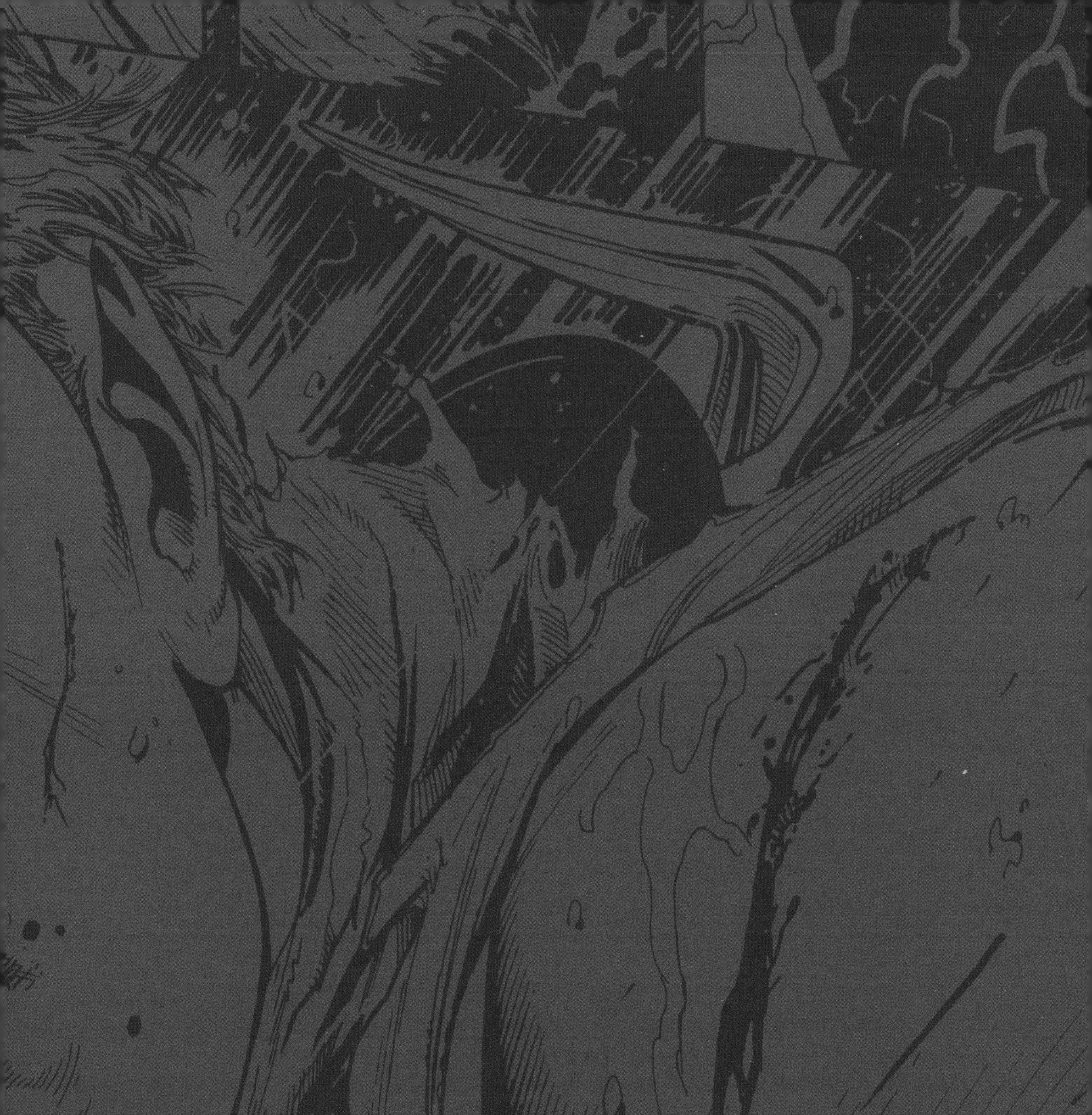

THE FLASH: REBIRTH

GEOFF **JOHNS** writer

ETHAN **VAN SCIVER** artist & covers

BRIAN **MILLER** of **HI-FI** ALEX **SINCLAIR** colorists

ROB **LEIGH** letterer

SCOTT **HANNA** additional inks on #6

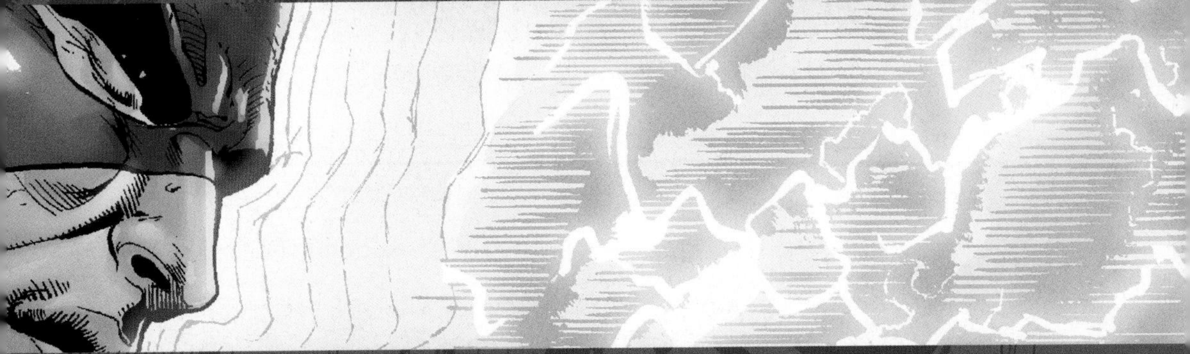

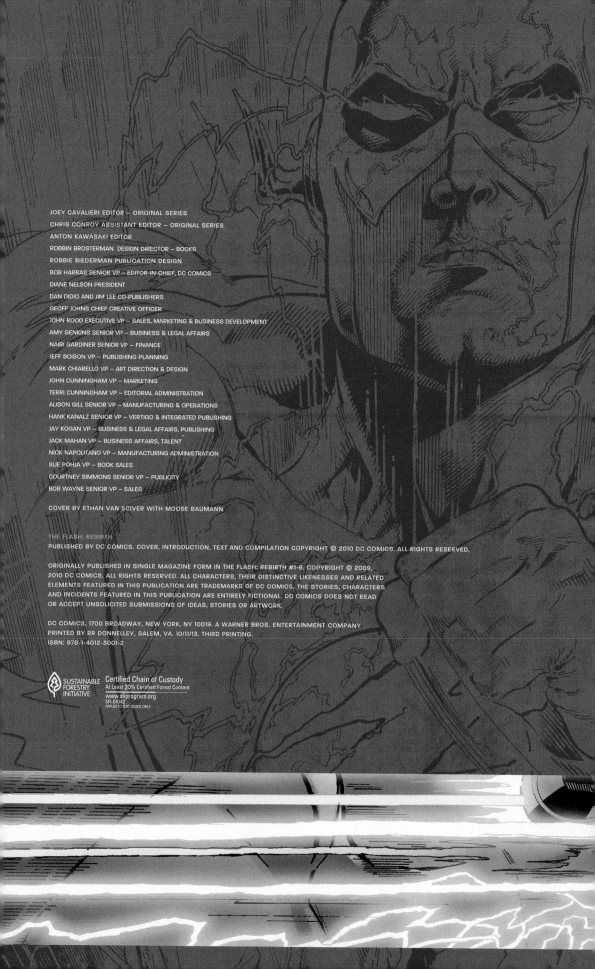

JOEY CAVALIERI EDITOR – ORIGINAL SERIES

CHRIS CONROY ASSISTANT EDITOR – ORIGINAL SERIES

ANTON KAWASAKI EDITOR

ROBBIN BROSTERMAN DESIGN DIRECTOR – BOOKS

ROBBIE BIEDERMAN PUBLICATION DESIGN

BOB HARRAS SENIOR VP – EDITOR-IN-CHIEF, DC COMICS

DIANE NELSON PRESIDENT

DAN DIDIO AND JIM LEE CO-PUBLISHERS

GEOFF JOHNS CHIEF CREATIVE OFFICER

JOHN ROOD EXECUTIVE VP – SALES, MARKETING & BUSINESS DEVELOPMENT

AMY GENKINS SENIOR VP – BUSINESS & LEGAL AFFAIRS

NAIRI GARDINER SENIOR VP – FINANCE

JEFF BOISON VP – PUBLISHING PLANNING

MARK CHIARELLO VP – ART DIRECTION & DESIGN

JOHN CUNNINGHAM VP – MARKETING

TERRI CUNNINGHAM VP – EDITORIAL ADMINISTRATION

ALISON GILL SENIOR VP – MANUFACTURING & OPERATIONS

HANK KANALZ SENIOR VP – VERTIGO & INTEGRATED PUBLISHING

JAY KOGAN VP – BUSINESS & LEGAL AFFAIRS, PUBLISHING

JACK MAHAN VP – BUSINESS AFFAIRS, TALENT

NICK NAPOLITANO VP – MANUFACTURING ADMINISTRATION

SUE POHJA VP – BOOK SALES

COURTNEY SIMMONS SENIOR VP – PUBLICITY

BOB WAYNE SENIOR VP – SALES

COVER BY ETHAN VAN SCIVER WITH MOOSE BAUMANN

SUSTAINABLE FORESTRY INITIATIVE

Certified Chain of Custody
At Least 20% Certified Forest Content
www.sfiprogram.org
SFI-01042
APPLIES TO TEXT STOCK ONLY

A FLASH FORWARD BY MATT CHERNISS

It's a funny thing about superheroes; keeping them dead is often harder than actually killing them in the first place. We want our fantasies to be grounded in reality, our character's flaws to be real, and their sacrifices to carry weight. Sometimes that means our favorite heroes must die. Those moments, rare as they are, remind us why we love our heroes. But that is where the conflict begins. Keeping them dead means not having the joy of reading them every month. Yet, in bringing them back to life, we run the risk of minimizing their heroism, the tragedy of their death, or the power of their sacrifice. We care too much about them to do that, either.

It's also true that the longer a character remains dead, the greater the importance and scrutiny is put on his return. A character who returns from death after being absent for 6 months or a year? His return is generally accompanied by a fanboy in the new arrivals section uttering, "I knew they'd bring him back." A beloved character who is absent for years on end? That is an event. Barry Allen's absence of 23 years most certainly falls into that category.

When you think about it, it's almost unfathomable Barry was gone as long as he was. This isn't some "B" grade superhero. This is an Icon. The character that launched the Silver Age in SHOWCASE #4, introduced us to the Multiverse in THE FLASH #123, and helped found the Justice League in THE BRAVE AND THE BOLD #28. A character with arguably one of the best two or three Rogues' Galleries in all of comics, and my favorite DC villain (more on that later). Twenty-three years! It makes Hal Jordan's 10-year absence seem like the blink of an eye.

I suppose one of the things that helped keep Barry out of the world of the living was what he died doing. Some heroes die saving a loved one, others save their beloved city, maybe even their home planet. Barry literally saved the entire Universe from being erased from existence. If a hero does that, and then just happens to show up a few months later, it would have surely minimized one of the seminal events in Comic Book History.

All that is to say this: If you are going to bring Barry Allen back, you better not screw it up. A satisfying hero's return is remembered fondly. A disastrous one becomes part of comic book lore. I don't even need to mention them by name, we all know which ones they are. We still complain about them to this day. That's a lot of responsibility for any writer to carry on their shoulders. Which leads me to my last reason Barry was gone for so long: we were waiting for the right writer to bring Barry back.

Over the past 23 years there have been many great writers, some of whom have written the Flash. Again, I don't need to name them. We all know who they are. We buy their books every month. But to take on this task, in my mind only Geoff had the ability, knowledge, and most importantly, the affinity for the character to take on the challenge and succeed. For both Geoff and myself, Barry Allen's death in CRISIS ON INFINITE EARTHS was one of those moments that came early in our introduction to comic books, and had an impact that would endear us to comics for years to come. These magical moments, more often than not, happen when you are young, and stay with you long after. In many genres, it would be sacrilege for a writer to continue someone else's story. In comic books, it is tradition. And I think it is for the best, because in many instances, that young boy whose imagination was captured by a single moment will take greater care of it than someone burdened by years of storytelling.

The fact that Geoff would approach THE FLASH: REBIRTH more as an honor than as a task also speaks to why he was the right person to tell this story. Barry's return wasn't the trickiest in terms of narrative. It was the emotional significance of Barry's return and the impact it would have on the DC universe that was most difficult. That is where Geoff's stories always stand out.

I'm also grateful that Reverse Flash found his way into the story as well. I'm not sure if it is the striking yellow costume, with the red lightning bolt/black circle insignia, or the fact that his villainy included the murder of Barry's wife, Iris, long before such things were done regularly in comics, but every time Reverse Flash graces a comic cover, I can't help but look inside.

No matter how strong, how fast, or how intelligent a super-hero is, they all share a common weakness. Every hero is susceptible to a bad story. It can bring them to their knees faster than any weapon or arch-nemesis. I have never read a bad story from Geoff, and THE FLASH: REBIRTH is no exception. Enjoy!

MATT CHERNISS
LOS ANGELES, CALIFORNIA JANUARY, 2010

Matt Cherniss is a TV Development Executive for the FOX Broadcasting Company, where he developed shows including *Glee* and *Human Target*. In his previous job at FX, he took part in the development of shows including *Nip/Tuck*, *Rescue Me*, *Sons of Anarchy*, *Damages*, and *It's Always Sunny in Philadelphia*. Outside of his day job, he is a part-time comic writer, and full-time comic fanatic.

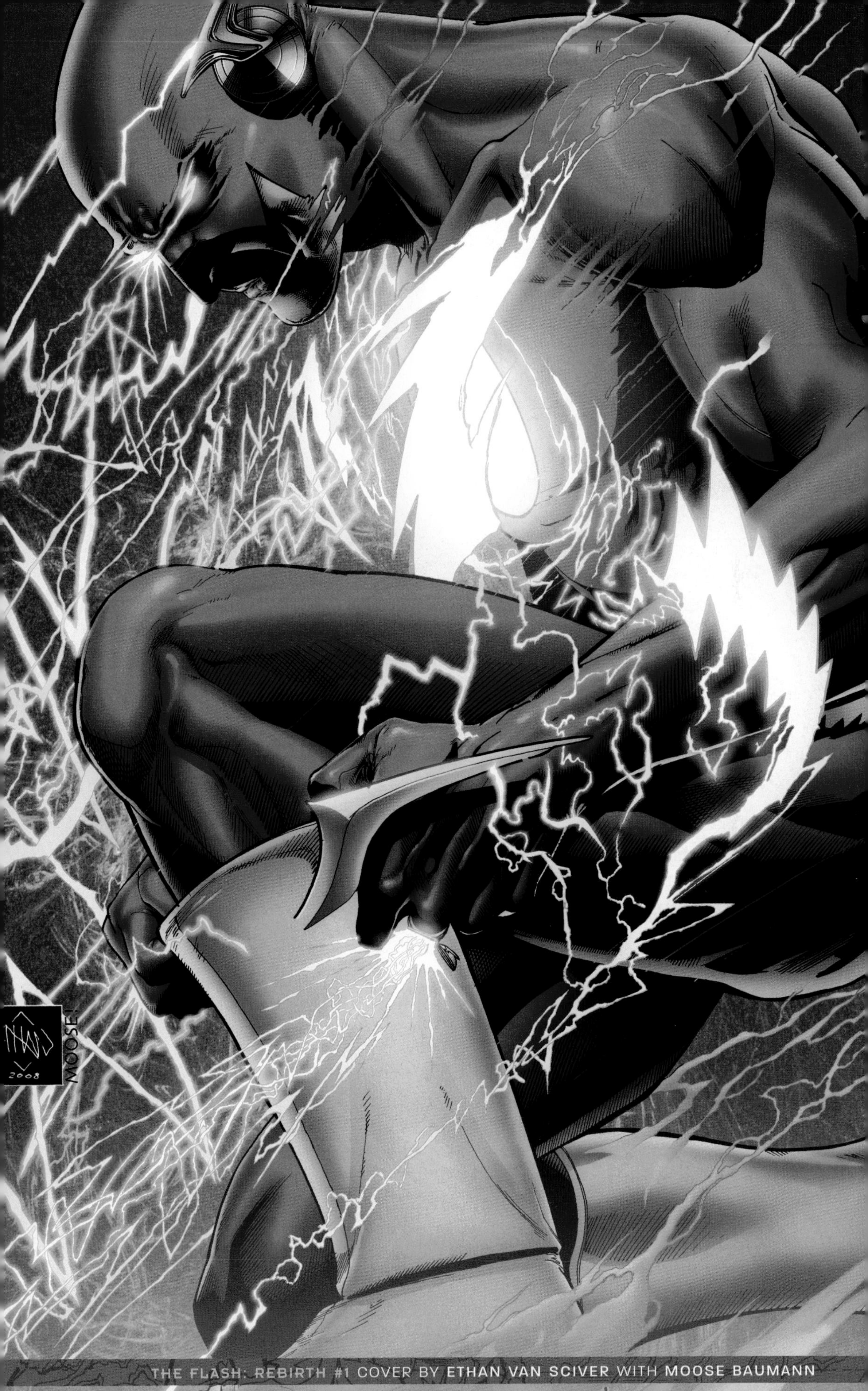
MOOSE!
2008

THE FLASH: REBIRTH #1 COVER BY ETHAN VAN SCIVER WITH MOOSE BAUMANN

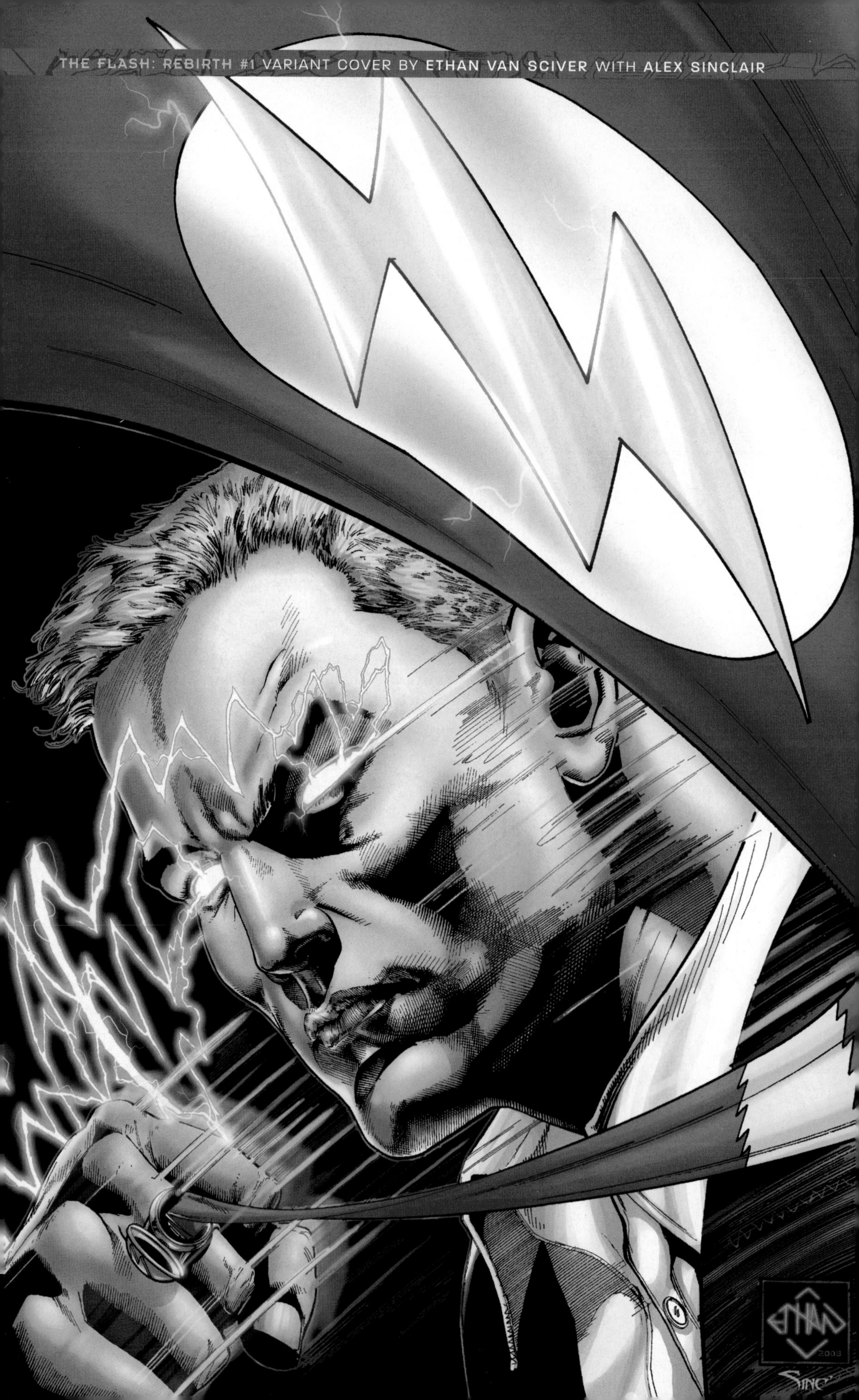

THE FLASH: REBIRTH #1 VARIANT COVER BY ETHAN VAN SCIVER WITH ALEX SINCLAIR

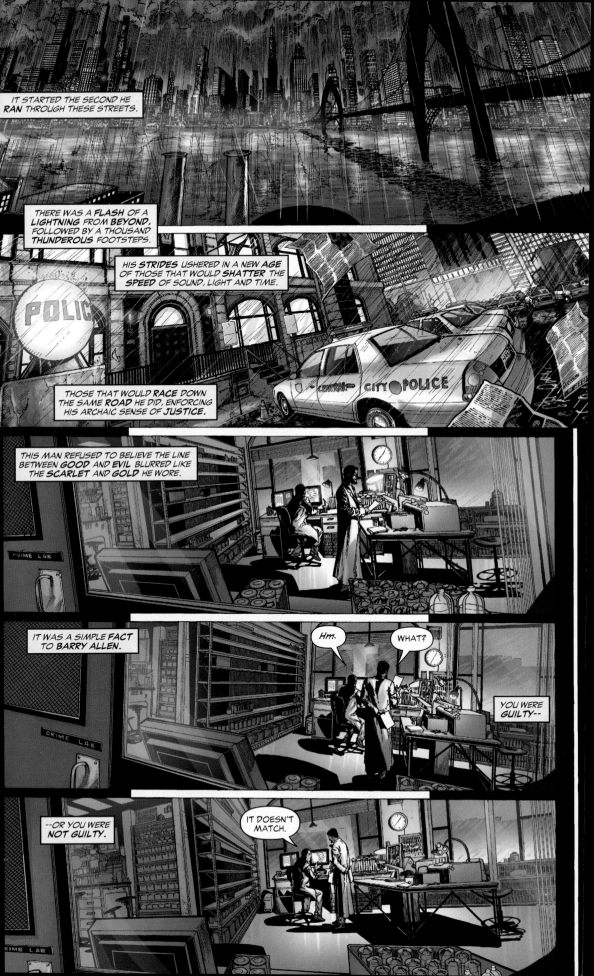

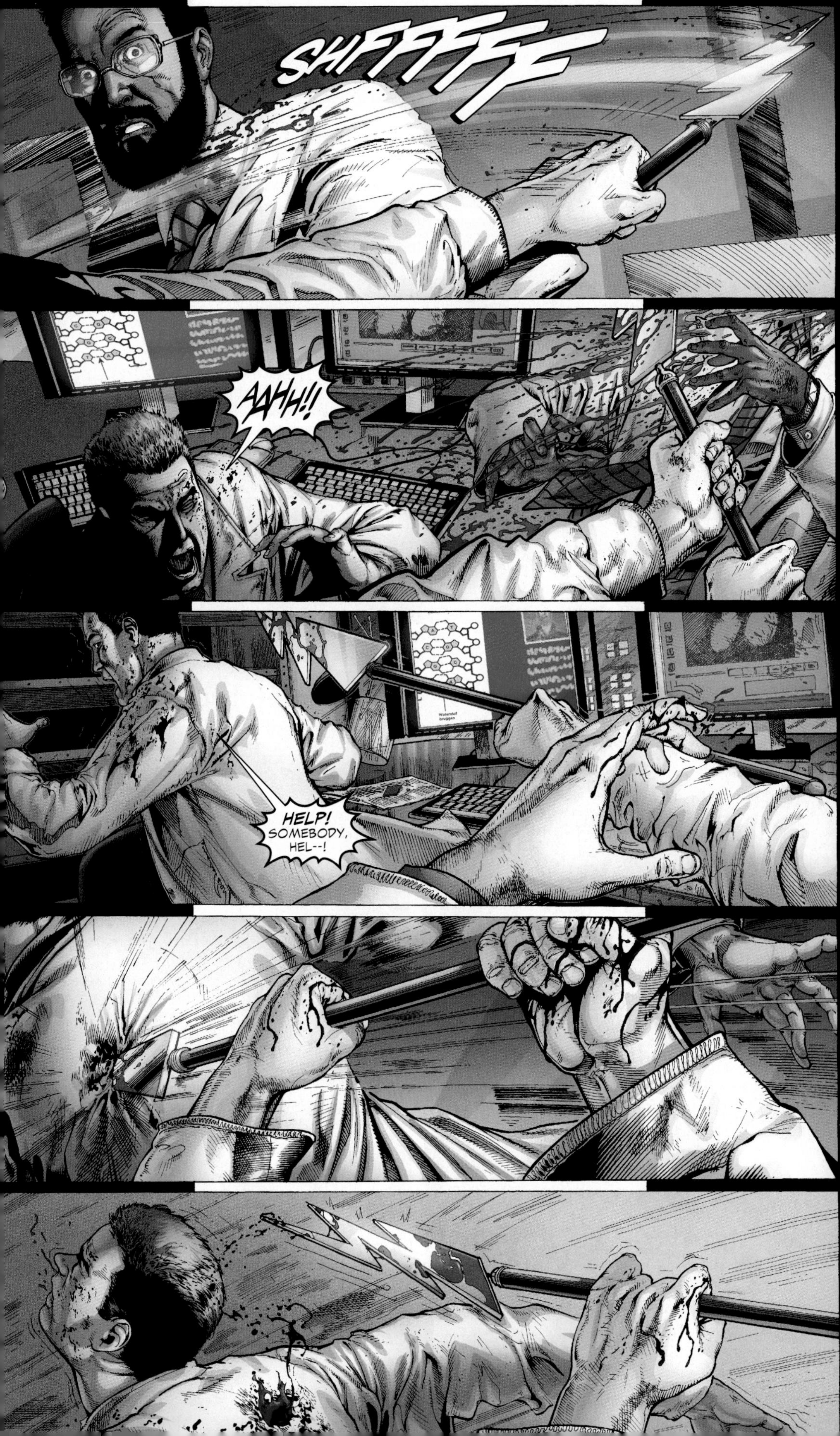

SHFFFFF
AAHH!!
HELP! SOMEBODY, HEL--!

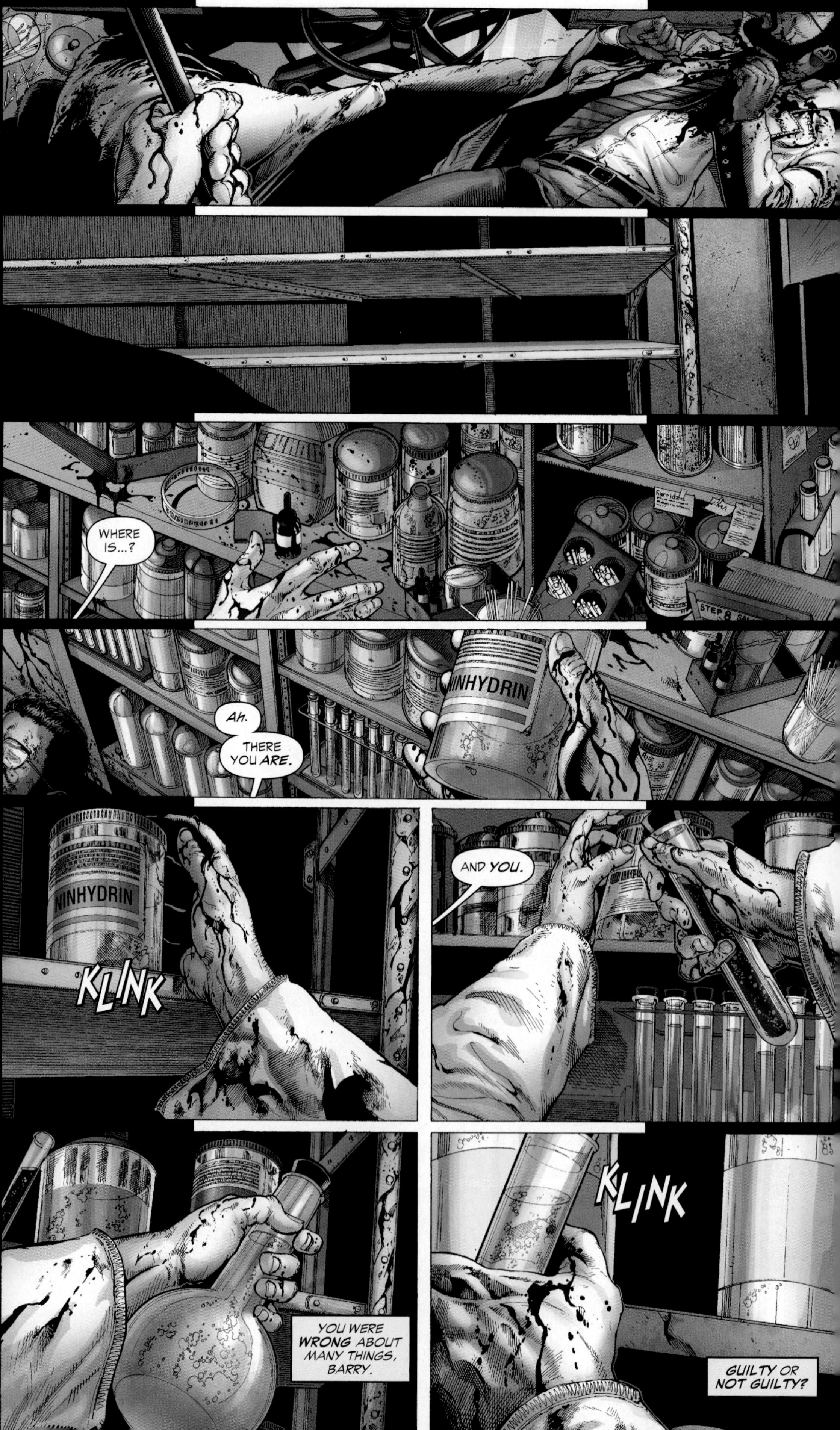
WHERE IS...?
NINHYDRIN
Ah.
THERE YOU ARE.
NINHYDRIN
KLINK
AND YOU.
KLINK
YOU WERE WRONG ABOUT MANY THINGS, BARRY.
GUILTY OR NOT GUILTY?

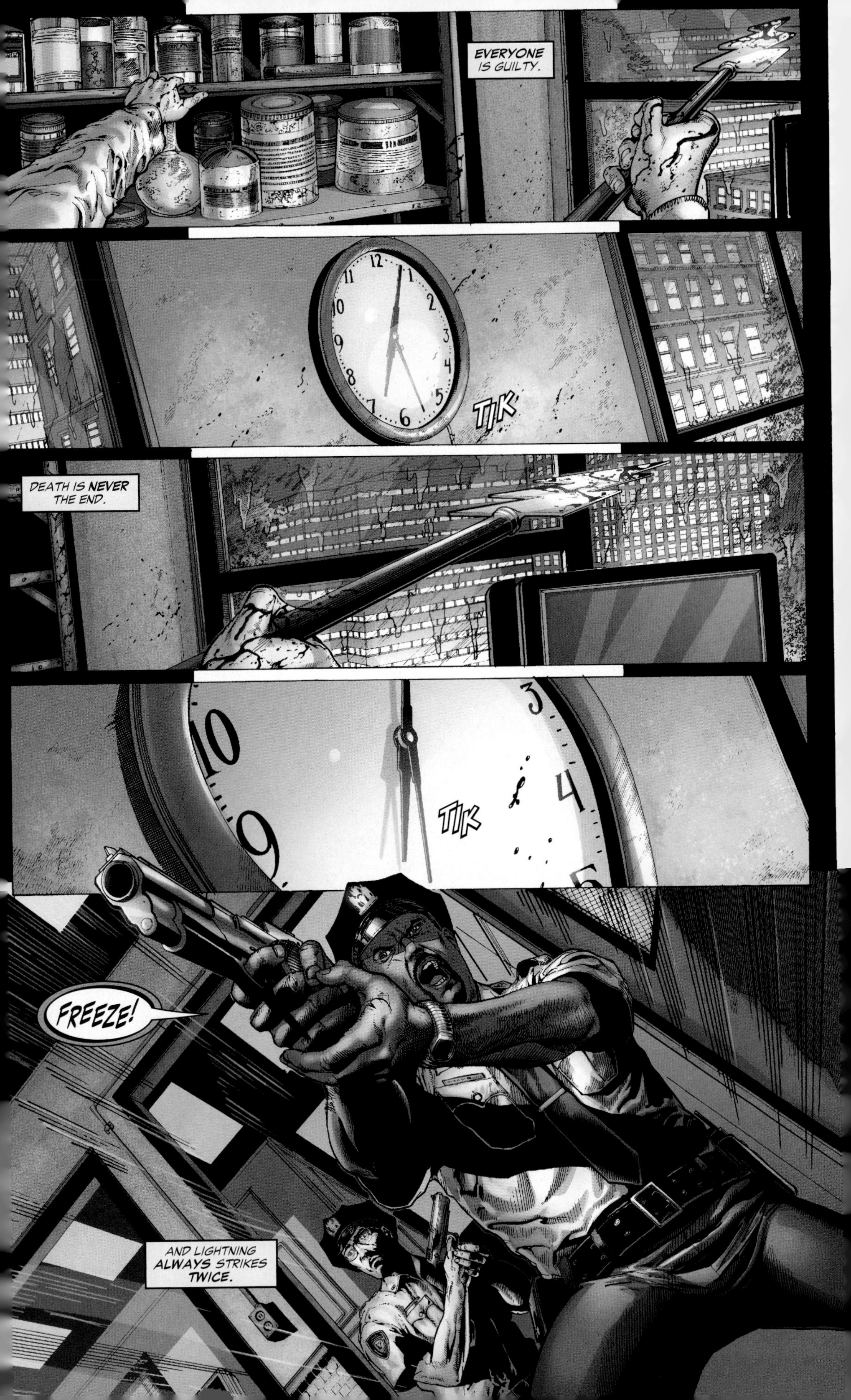
EVERYONE IS GUILTY.
TIK
DEATH IS NEVER THE END.
TIK
FREEZE!
AND LIGHTNING ALWAYS STRIKES TWICE.

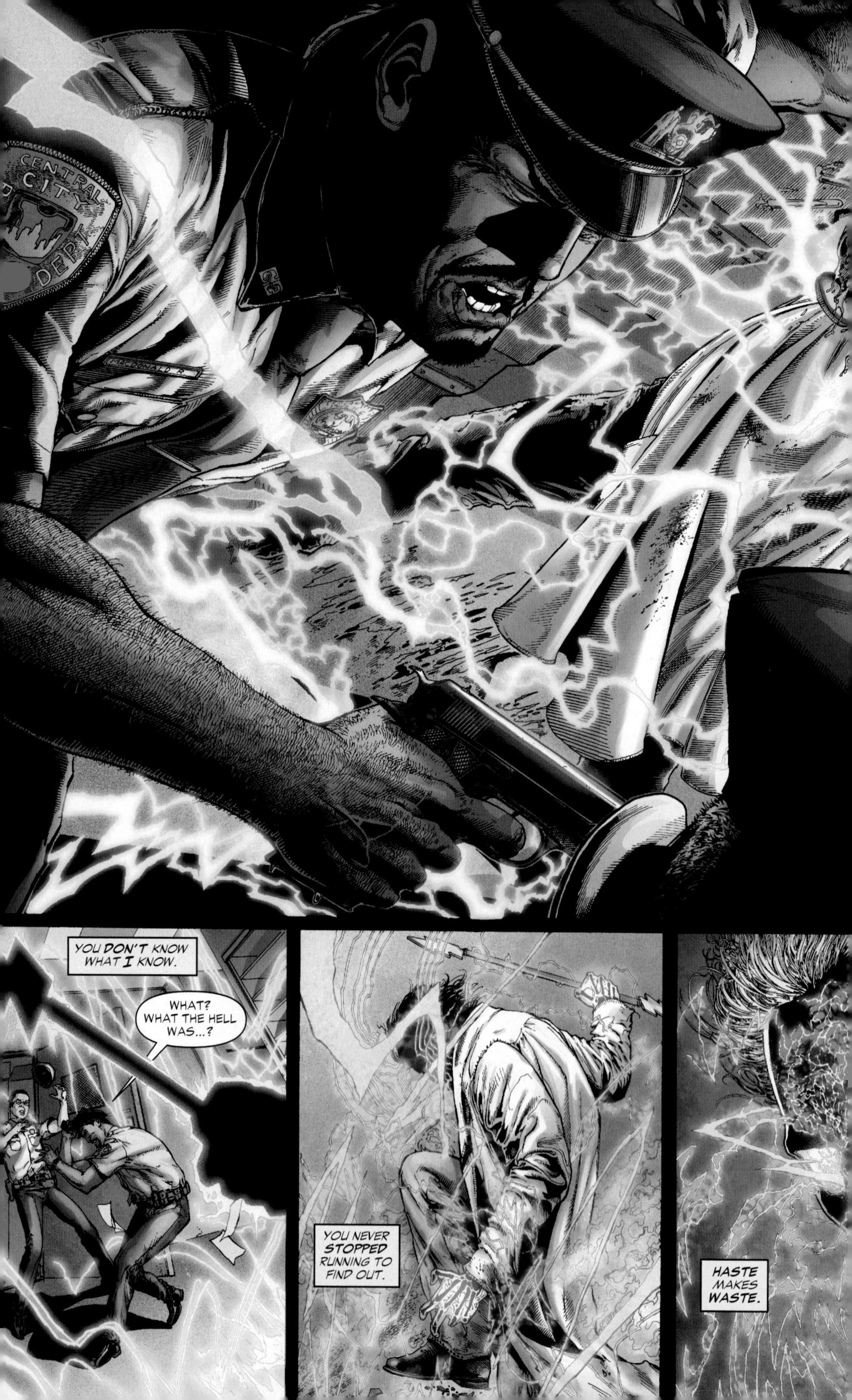
YOU **DON'T** KNOW WHAT **I** KNOW.
WHAT? WHAT THE HELL WAS...?
YOU NEVER **STOPPED** RUNNING TO FIND OUT.
HASTE MAKES **WASTE.**

SRAAAAAK

LOTS OF WASTE.

I BROUGHT YOU BACK, BARRY--

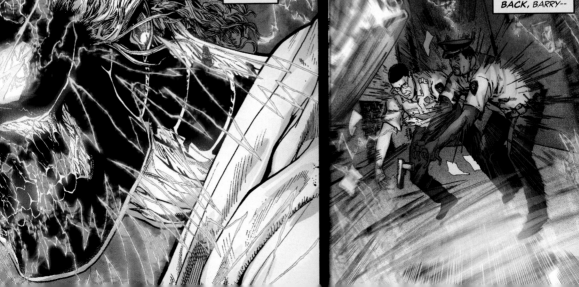

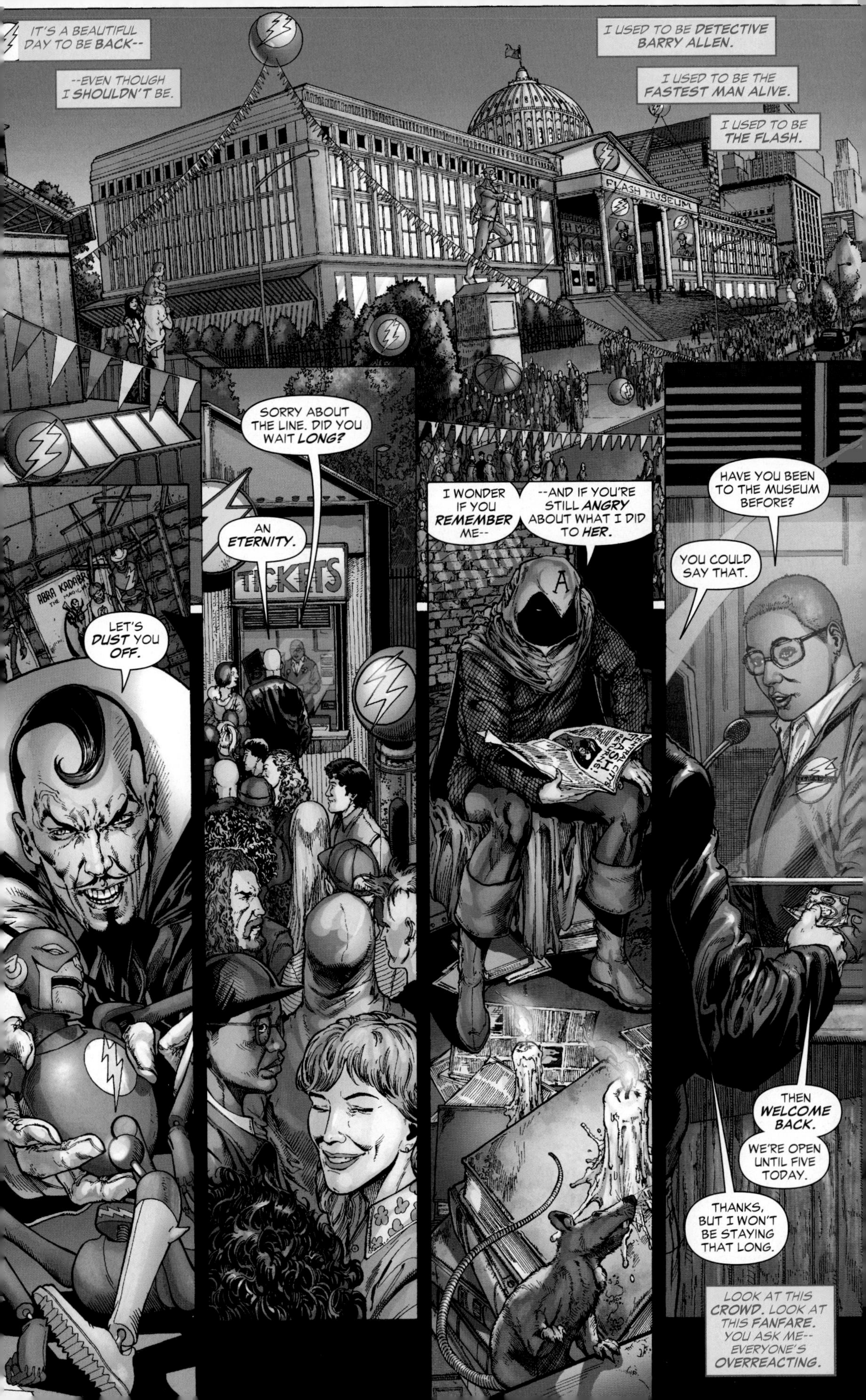

IT'S A BEAUTIFUL DAY TO BE BACK--
--EVEN THOUGH I SHOULDN'T BE.
I USED TO BE DETECTIVE BARRY ALLEN.
I USED TO BE THE FASTEST MAN ALIVE.
I USED TO BE THE FLASH.
FLASH MUSEUM
ABRA KADABRA
LET'S DUST YOU OFF.
SORRY ABOUT THE LINE. DID YOU WAIT LONG?
AN ETERNITY.
TICKETS
I WONDER IF YOU REMEMBER ME--
--AND IF YOU'RE STILL ANGRY ABOUT WHAT I DID TO HER.
HAVE YOU BEEN TO THE MUSEUM BEFORE?
YOU COULD SAY THAT.
THEN WELCOME BACK.
WE'RE OPEN UNTIL FIVE TODAY.
THANKS, BUT I WON'T BE STAYING THAT LONG.
LOOK AT THIS CROWD. LOOK AT THIS FANFARE. YOU ASK ME-- EVERYONE'S OVERREACTING.

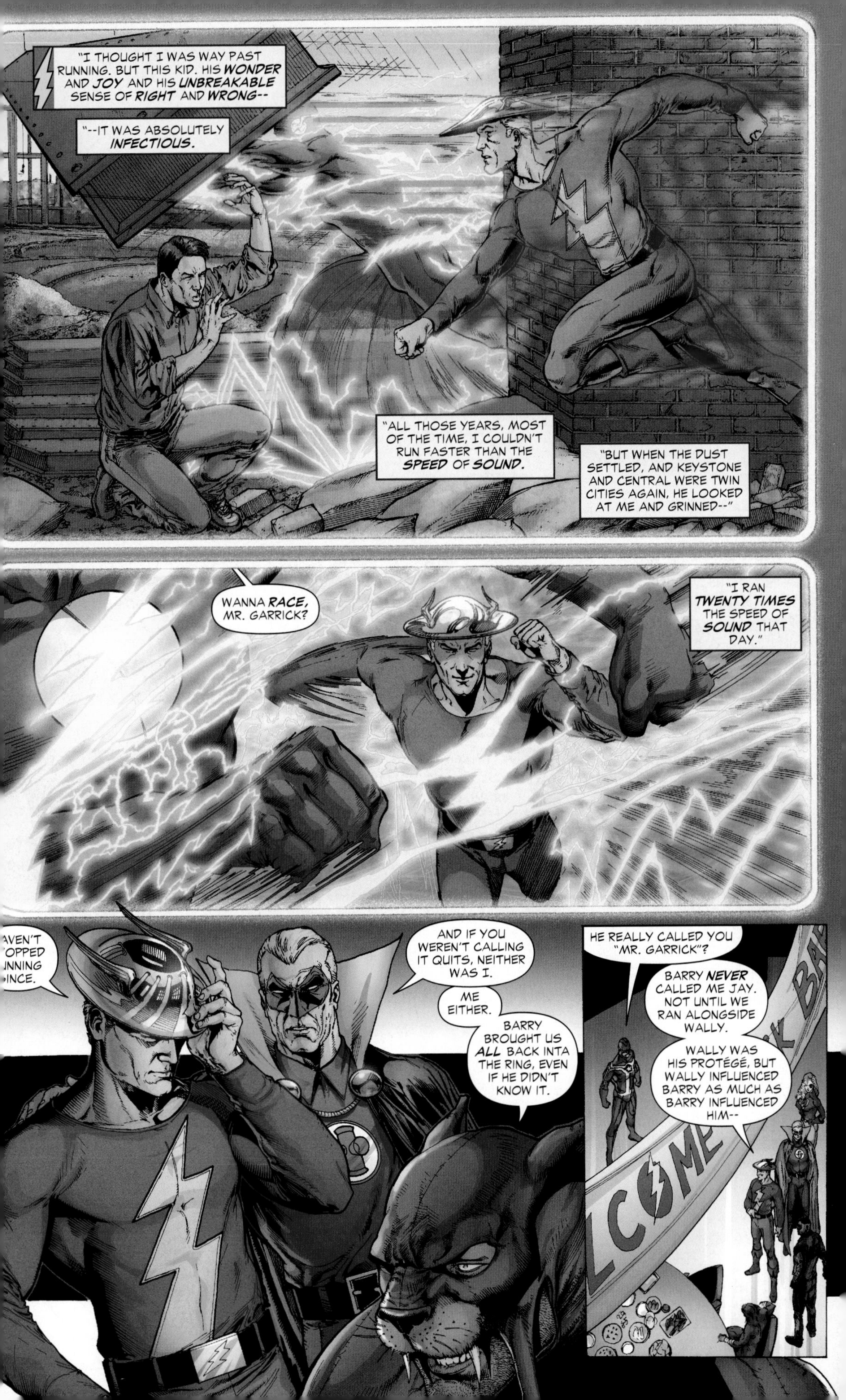
"I THOUGHT I WAS WAY PAST RUNNING. BUT THIS KID. HIS WONDER AND JOY AND HIS UNBREAKABLE SENSE OF RIGHT AND WRONG--
"--IT WAS ABSOLUTELY INFECTIOUS.
"ALL THOSE YEARS, MOST OF THE TIME, I COULDN'T RUN FASTER THAN THE SPEED OF SOUND.
"BUT WHEN THE DUST SETTLED, AND KEYSTONE AND CENTRAL WERE TWIN CITIES AGAIN, HE LOOKED AT ME AND GRINNED--"
WANNA RACE, MR. GARRICK?
"I RAN TWENTY TIMES THE SPEED OF SOUND THAT DAY."
AVEN'T OPPED UNNING INCE.
AND IF YOU WEREN'T CALLING IT QUITS, NEITHER WAS I.
ME EITHER.
BARRY BROUGHT US ALL BACK INTA THE RING, EVEN IF HE DIDN'T KNOW IT.
HE REALLY CALLED YOU "MR. GARRICK"?
BARRY NEVER CALLED ME JAY. NOT UNTIL WE RAN ALONGSIDE WALLY.
WALLY WAS HIS PROTÉGÉ, BUT WALLY INFLUENCED BARRY AS MUCH AS BARRY INFLUENCED HIM--

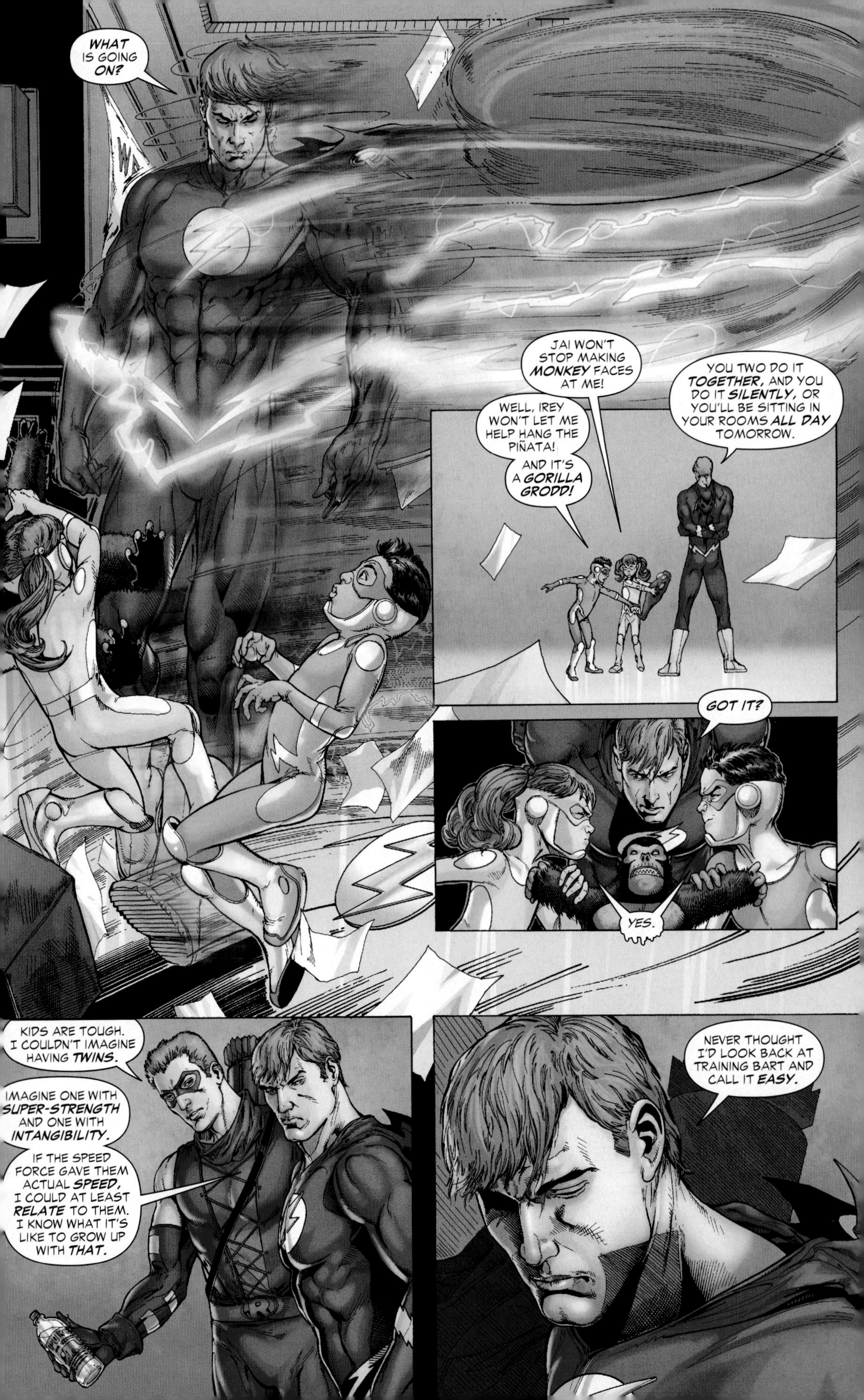
WHAT IS GOING ON?
JAI WON'T STOP MAKING MONKEY FACES AT ME!
WELL, IREY WON'T LET ME HELP HANG THE PIÑATA!
AND IT'S A GORILLA GRODD!
YOU TWO DO IT TOGETHER, AND YOU DO IT SILENTLY, OR YOU'LL BE SITTING IN YOUR ROOMS ALL DAY TOMORROW.
GOT IT?
YES.
KIDS ARE TOUGH. I COULDN'T IMAGINE HAVING TWINS.
IMAGINE ONE WITH SUPER-STRENGTH AND ONE WITH INTANGIBILITY.
IF THE SPEED FORCE GAVE THEM ACTUAL SPEED, I COULD AT LEAST RELATE TO THEM. I KNOW WHAT IT'S LIKE TO GROW UP WITH THAT.
NEVER THOUGHT I'D LOOK BACK AT TRAINING BART AND CALL IT EASY.

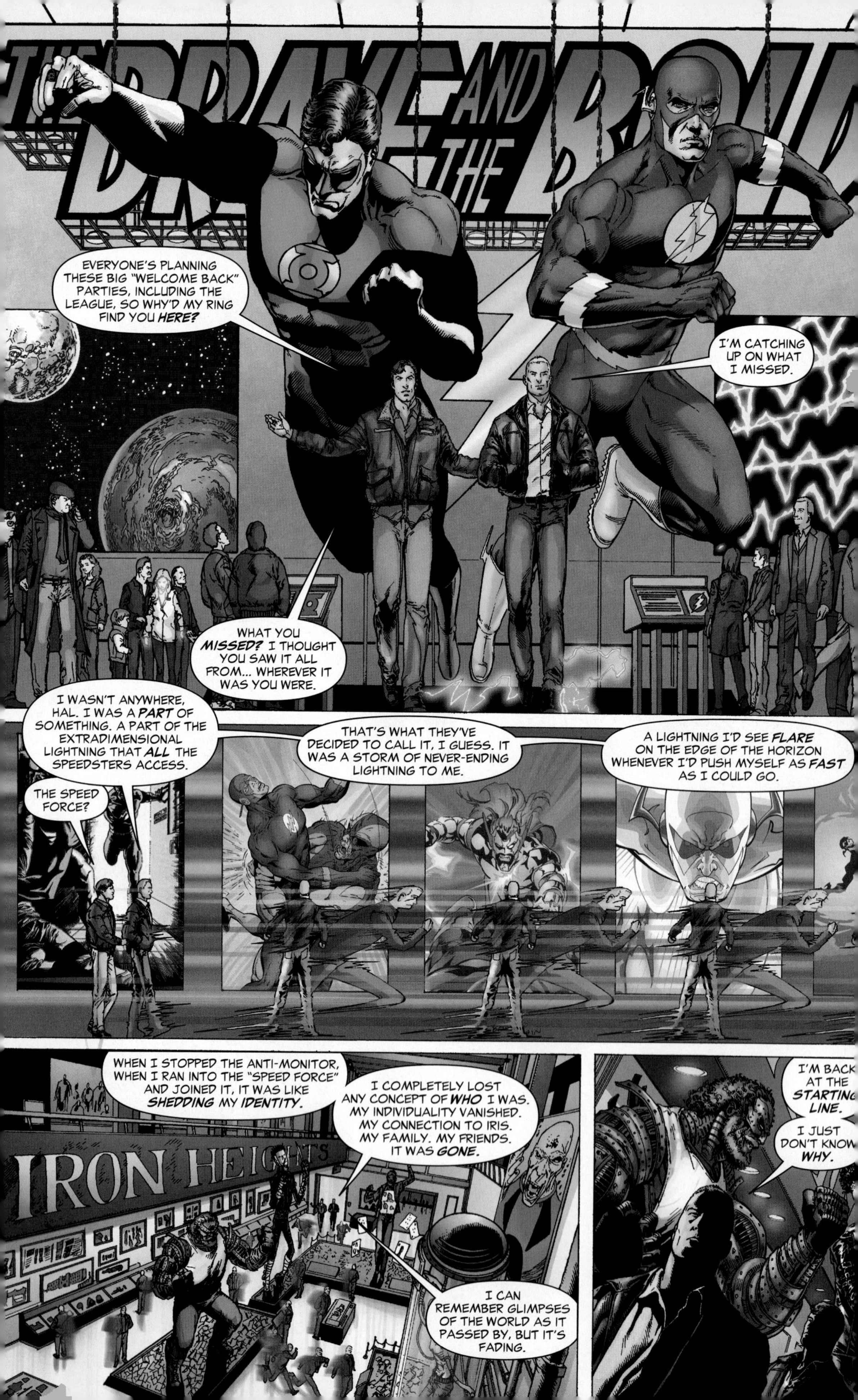
THE BRAVE AND THE BOLD
EVERYONE'S PLANNING THESE BIG "WELCOME BACK" PARTIES, INCLUDING THE LEAGUE, SO WHY'D MY RING FIND YOU HERE?
I'M CATCHING UP ON WHAT I MISSED.
WHAT YOU MISSED? I THOUGHT YOU SAW IT ALL FROM... WHEREVER IT WAS YOU WERE.
I WASN'T ANYWHERE, HAL. I WAS A PART OF SOMETHING. A PART OF THE EXTRADIMENSIONAL LIGHTNING THAT ALL THE SPEEDSTERS ACCESS.
THE SPEED FORCE?
THAT'S WHAT THEY'VE DECIDED TO CALL IT, I GUESS. IT WAS A STORM OF NEVER-ENDING LIGHTNING TO ME.
A LIGHTNING I'D SEE FLARE ON THE EDGE OF THE HORIZON WHENEVER I'D PUSH MYSELF AS FAST AS I COULD GO.
WHEN I STOPPED THE ANTI-MONITOR, WHEN I RAN INTO THE "SPEED FORCE" AND JOINED IT, IT WAS LIKE SHEDDING MY IDENTITY.
I COMPLETELY LOST ANY CONCEPT OF WHO I WAS. MY INDIVIDUALITY VANISHED. MY CONNECTION TO IRIS. MY FAMILY. MY FRIENDS. IT WAS GONE.
IRON HEIGHTS
I CAN REMEMBER GLIMPSES OF THE WORLD AS IT PASSED BY, BUT IT'S FADING.
I'M BACK AT THE STARTING LINE.
I JUST DON'T KNOW WHY.

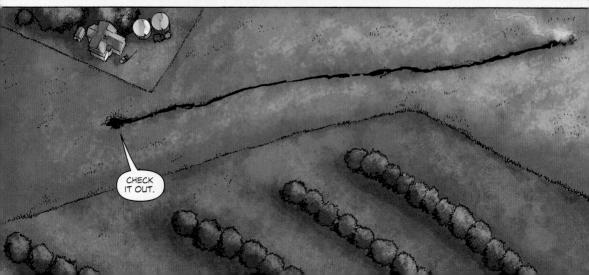

IT SMELLS LIKE BURNING RUBBER. WHAT IS IT?
I DON'T KNOW.
BUT WHATEVER IT IS...
...I THINK IT'S DEAD.
"YOU BEAT THE GRIM REAPER, BARRY."

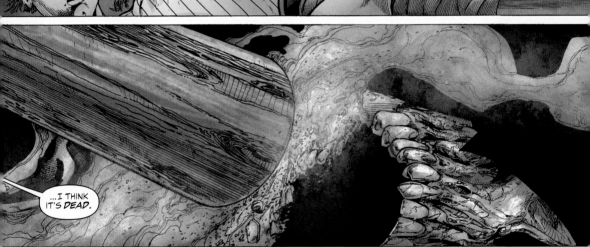

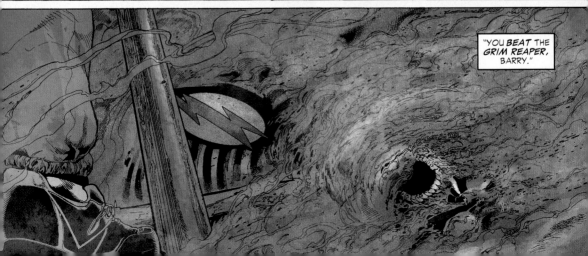

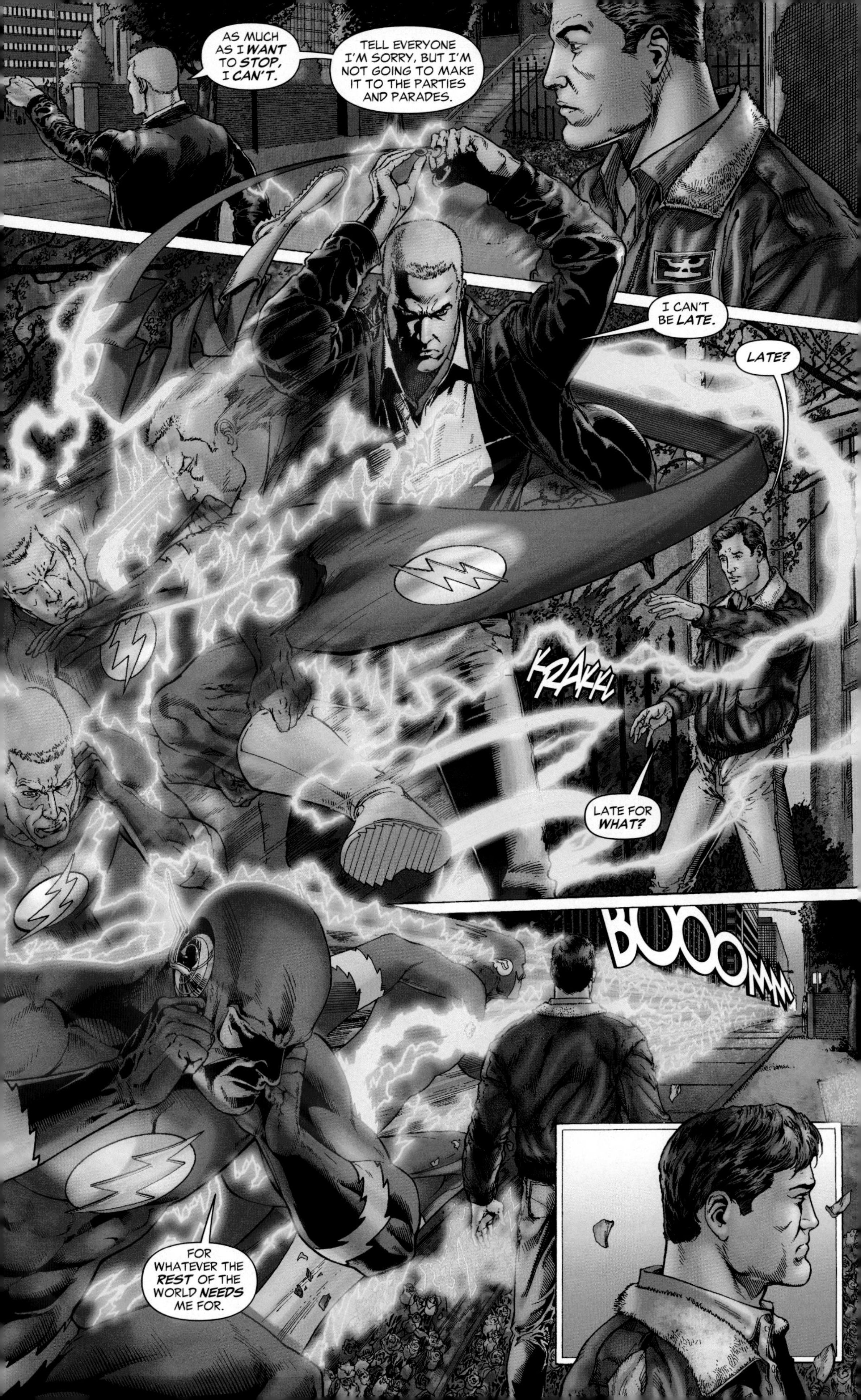

AS MUCH AS I WANT TO STOP, I CAN'T.
TELL EVERYONE I'M SORRY, BUT I'M NOT GOING TO MAKE IT TO THE PARTIES AND PARADES.
I CAN'T BE LATE.
LATE?
KRAKK!
LATE FOR WHAT?
BOOOMM
FOR WHATEVER THE REST OF THE WORLD NEEDS ME FOR.

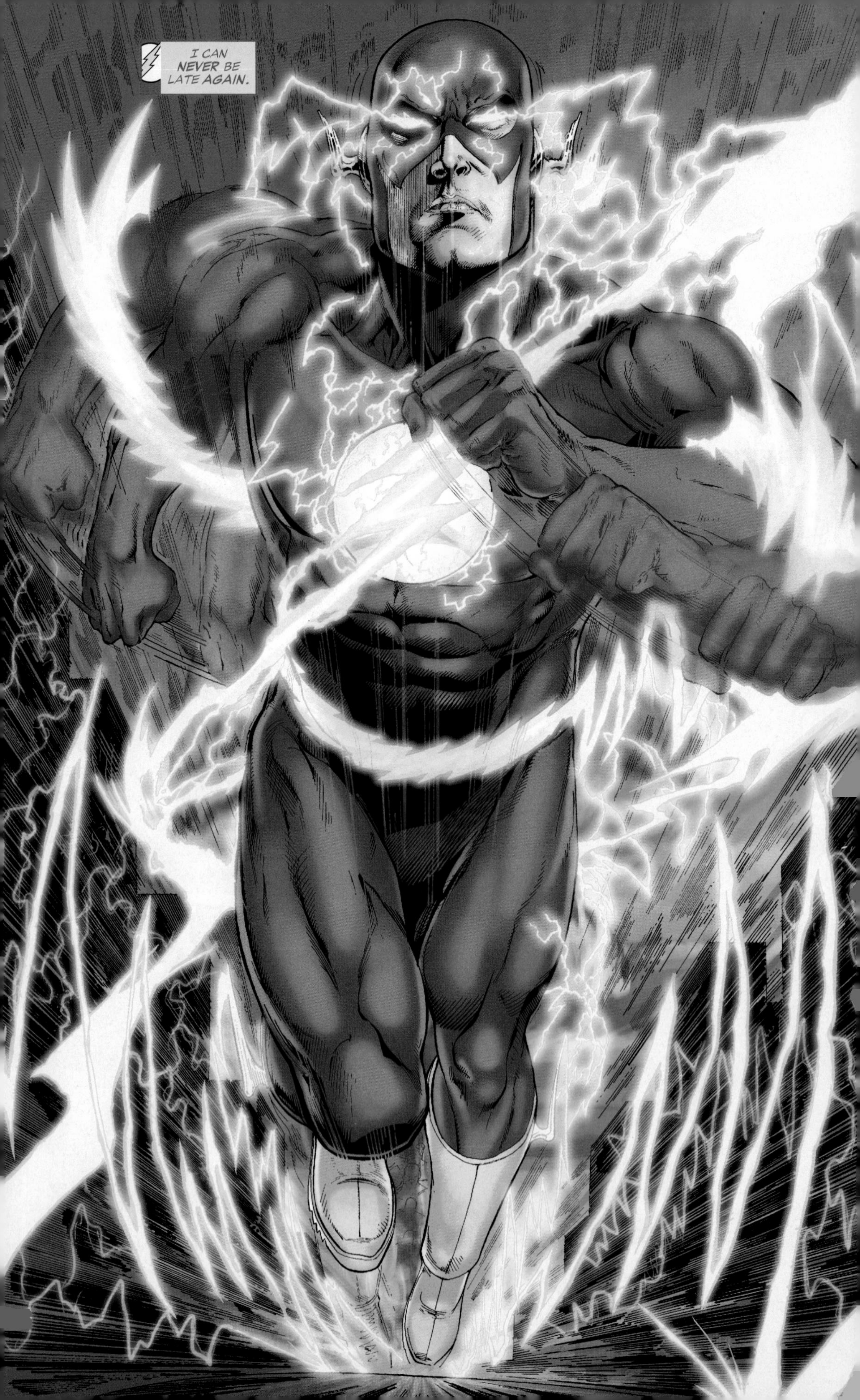
I CAN NEVER BE LATE AGAIN.

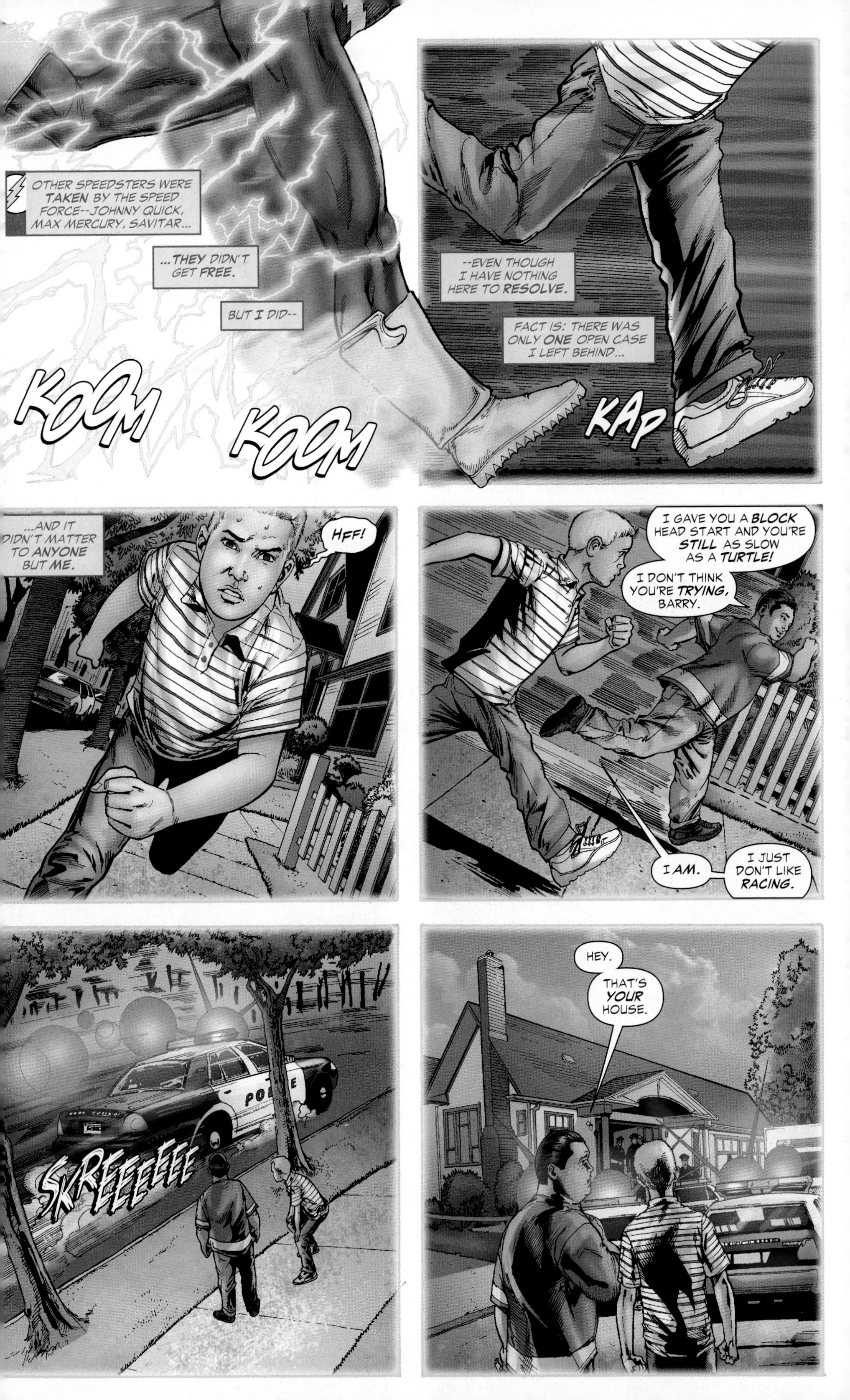
OTHER SPEEDSTERS WERE TAKEN BY THE SPEED FORCE--JOHNNY QUICK, MAX MERCURY, SAVITAR...
...THEY DIDN'T GET FREE.
BUT I DID--
KOOM
KOOM
--EVEN THOUGH I HAVE NOTHING HERE TO RESOLVE.
FACT IS: THERE WAS ONLY ONE OPEN CASE I LEFT BEHIND...
KAP
...AND IT DIDN'T MATTER TO ANYONE BUT ME.
HFF!
I GAVE YOU A BLOCK HEAD START AND YOU'RE STILL AS SLOW AS A TURTLE!
I DON'T THINK YOU'RE TRYING, BARRY.
I AM.
I JUST DON'T LIKE RACING.
SKREEEEEEE
HEY.
THAT'S YOUR HOUSE.

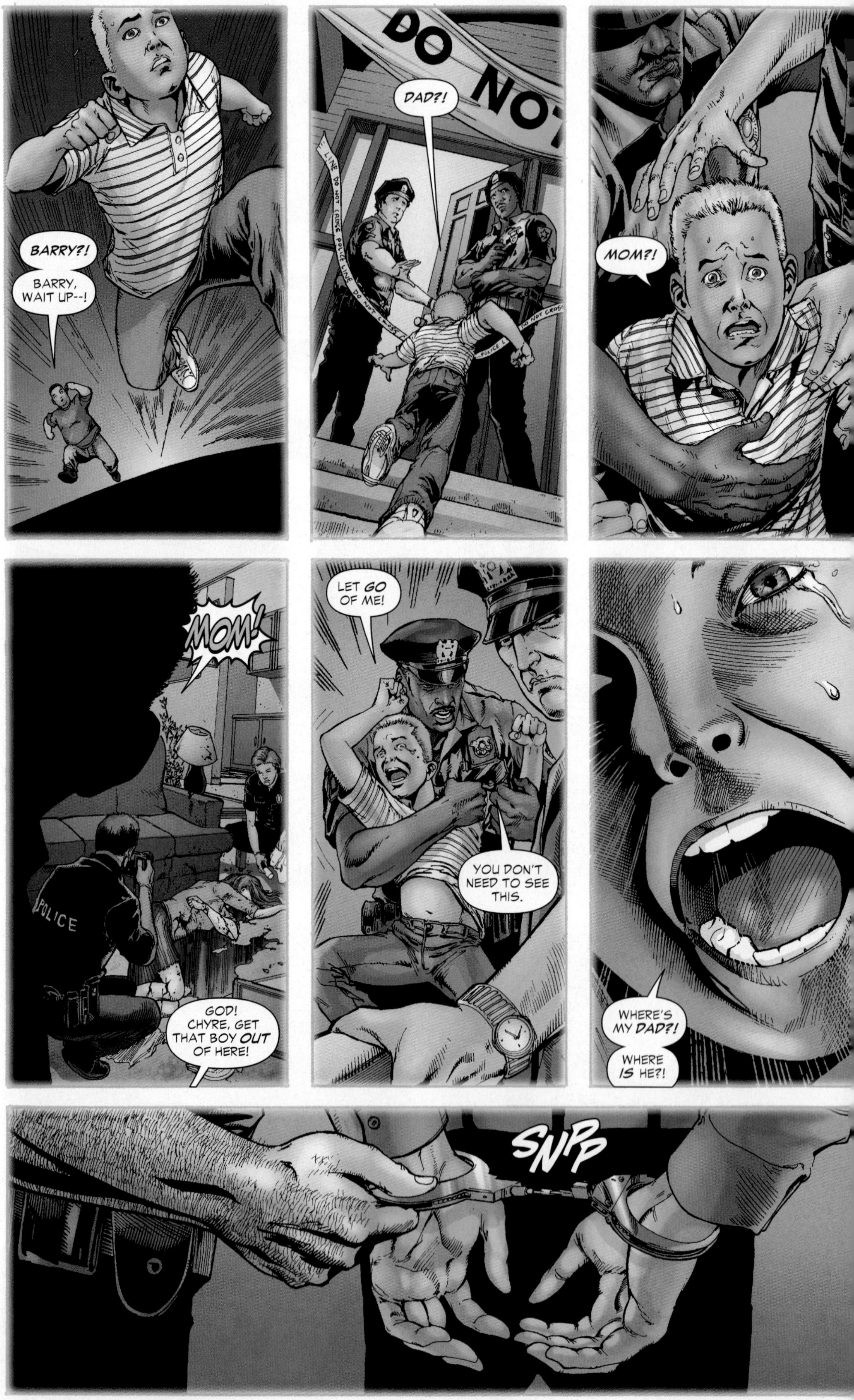
BARRY?!
BARRY, WAIT UP--!
DO NOT
DAD?!
MOM?!
MOM!
POLICE
GOD! CHYRE, GET THAT BOY OUT OF HERE!
LET GO OF ME!
YOU DON'T NEED TO SEE THIS.
WHERE'S MY DAD?!
WHERE IS HE?!
SNPP

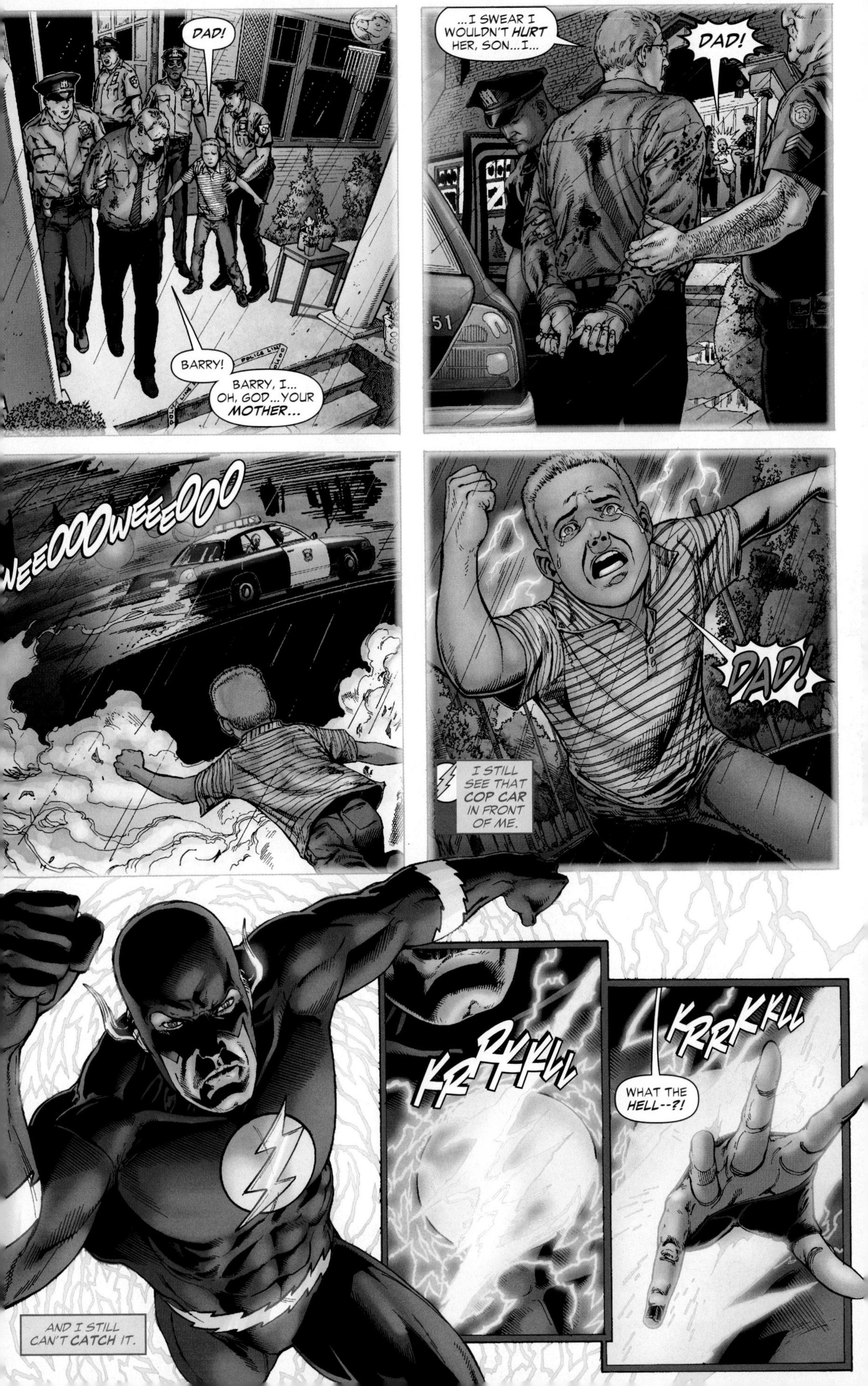
DAD!
BARRY!
BARRY, I... OH, GOD...YOUR MOTHER...
...I SWEAR I WOULDN'T HURT HER, SON...I...
DAD!
WEEOOOWEEEOOO
DAD!
I STILL SEE THAT COP CAR IN FRONT OF ME.
AND I STILL CAN'T CATCH IT.
KRRKKLL
KRRKKLL
WHAT THE HELL--?!

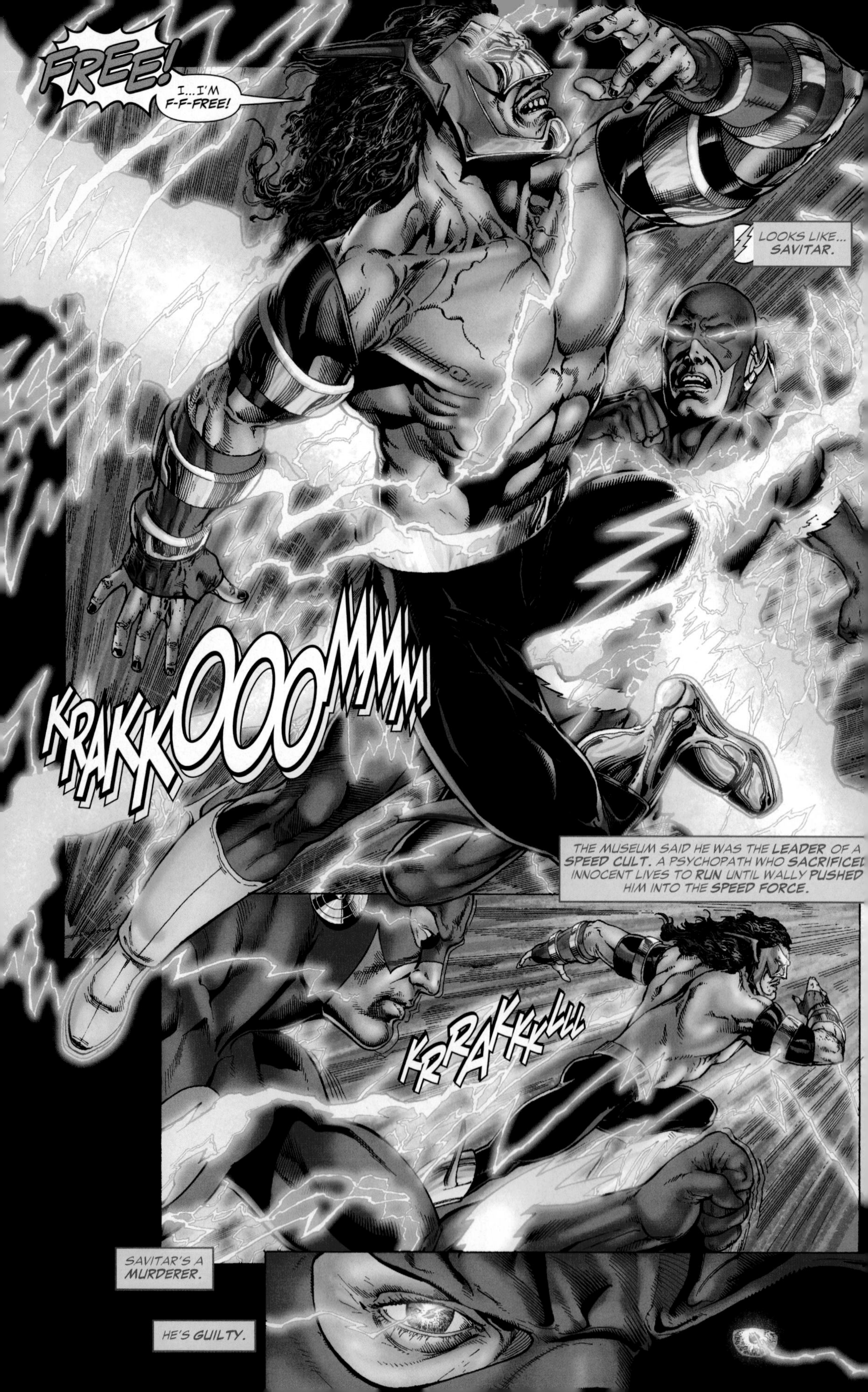
FREE!
I...I'M F-F-FREE!
LOOKS LIKE... SAVITAR.
KRAKKOOOOMMM
THE MUSEUM SAID HE WAS THE LEADER OF A SPEED CULT. A PSYCHOPATH WHO SACRIFICED INNOCENT LIVES TO RUN UNTIL WALLY PUSHED HIM INTO THE SPEED FORCE.
KRRAKKKLLL
SAVITAR'S A MURDERER.
HE'S GUILTY.

AND HE'S ON THE RUN.

I'M NOT SURE *HOW* YOU ESCAPED, BUT YOU'RE ABOUT TO WISH YOU *HADN'T*.

STAY *AWAY* FROM ME!

WHICH ONE OF YOU IS GOING TO TAKE *RESPONSIBILITY* FOR THIS?

NOT *ME!*

YOU KNOW MY NEPHEW, BUT *WE* HAVEN'T MET. WHY DON'T WE *PULL OVER* AND GET ACQUAINTED?

KK

KRRKKLL

AAAAHHH!

WALLY?!

KRRKKLL

YOU...

SOME KIND OF FEEDBACK.

I CAN'T SLOW DOWN.

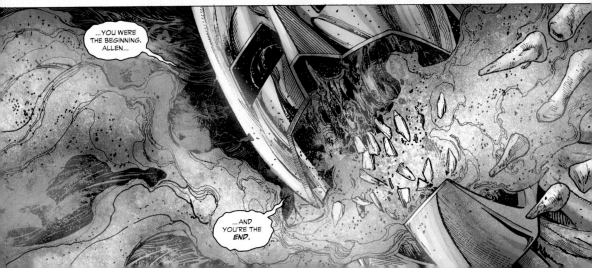

...YOU WERE THE BEGINNING, ALLEN...

...AND YOU'RE THE *END*.

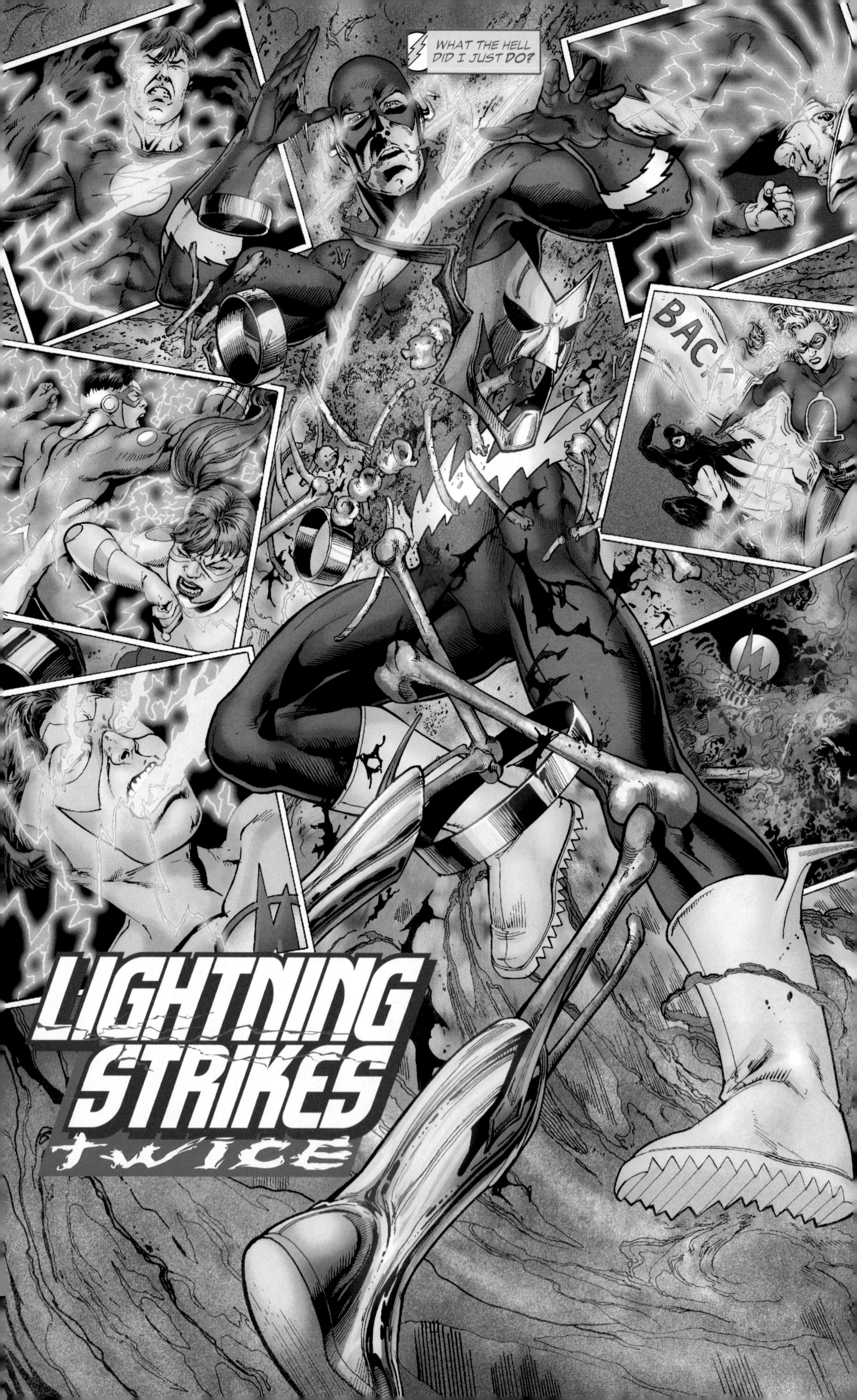
WHAT THE HELL
DID I JUST DO?
BACK
LIGHTNING
STRIKES
TWICE

THE FLASH: REBIRTH #2

COVER BY **ETHAN VAN SCIVER** (AFTER **CARMINE INFANTINO**) WITH **ALEX SINCLAIR**

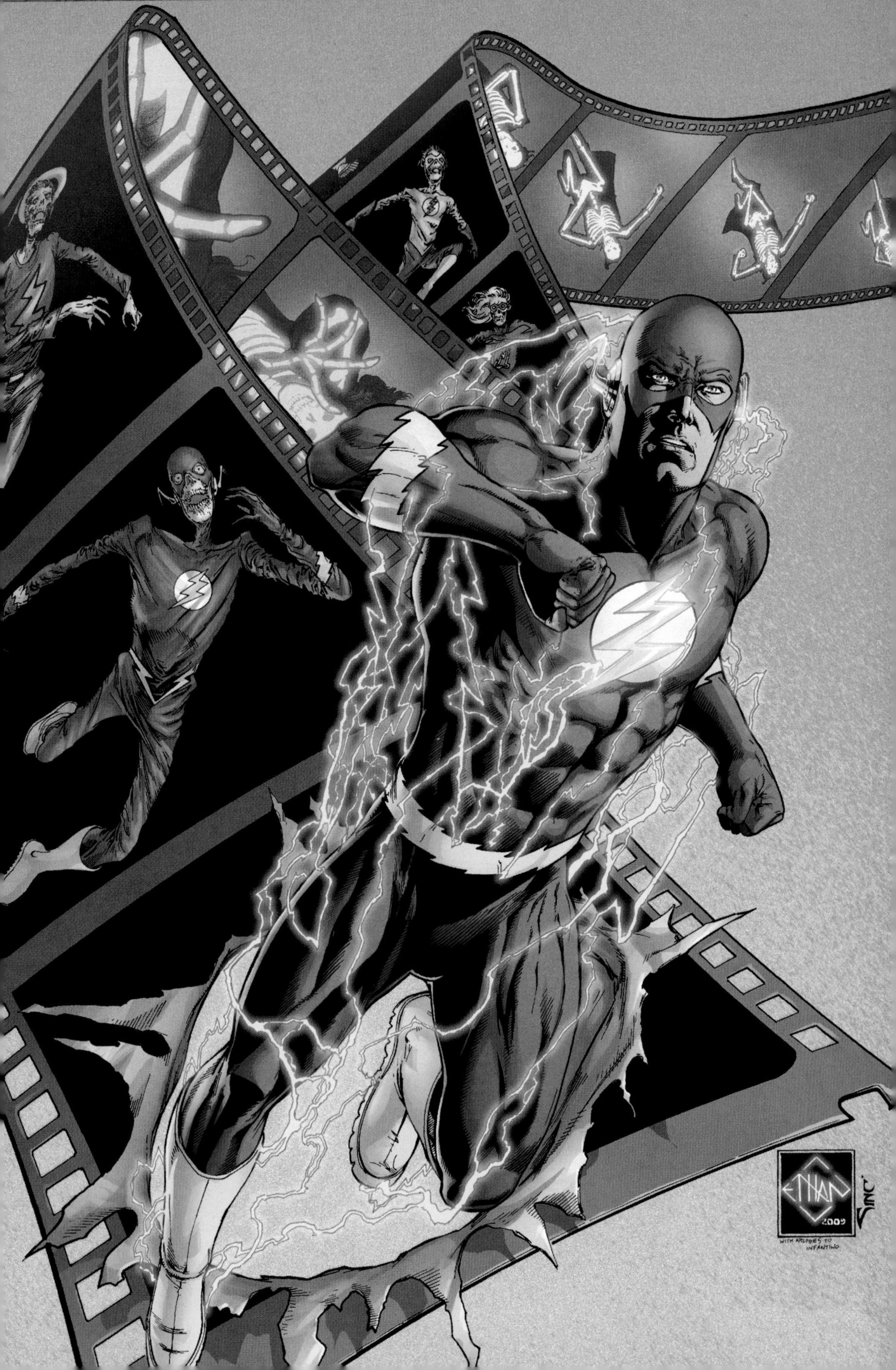
ETHAN
2009
WITH APOLOGIES TO INFANTINO

THE FLASH: REBIRTH #2 VARIANT COVER BY **ETHAN VAN SCIVER** WITH **ALEX SINCLAIR**

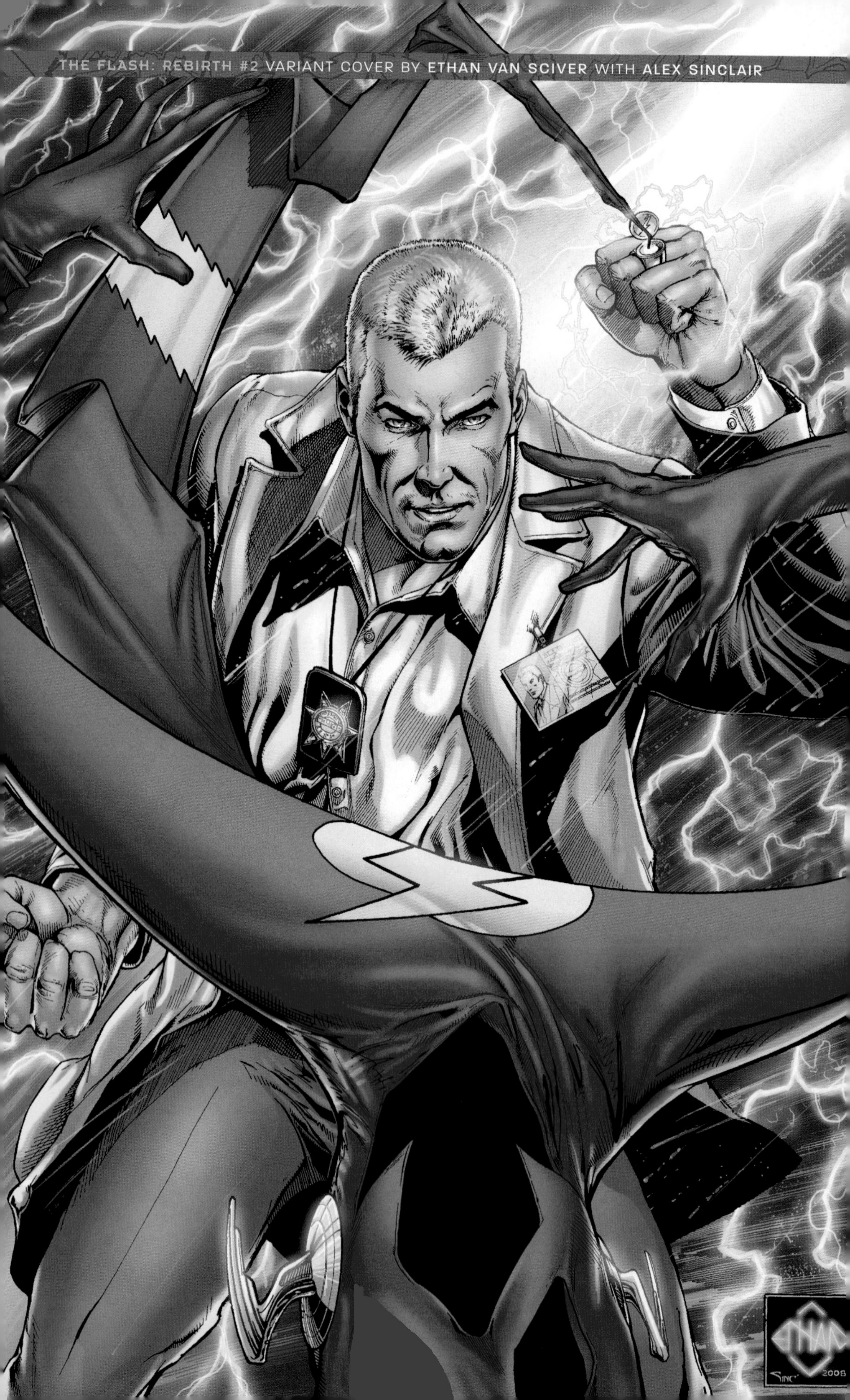

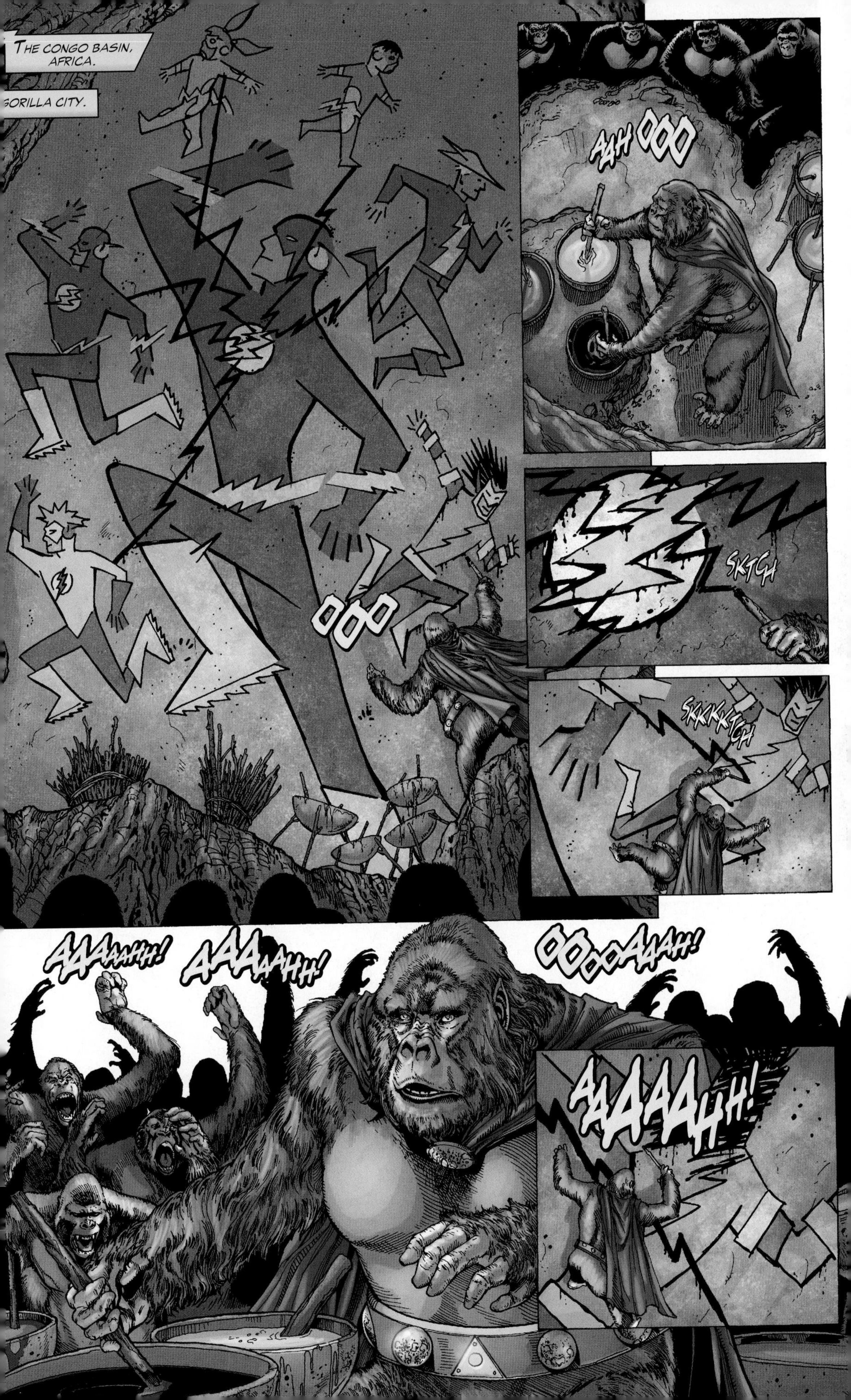

THE CONGO BASIN, AFRICA.
GORILLA CITY.
AAH OOO
OOO
SKTCH
SKKKKTCH
AAAaahh!
AAAaahh!
OOooAaah!
AAAAAHH!

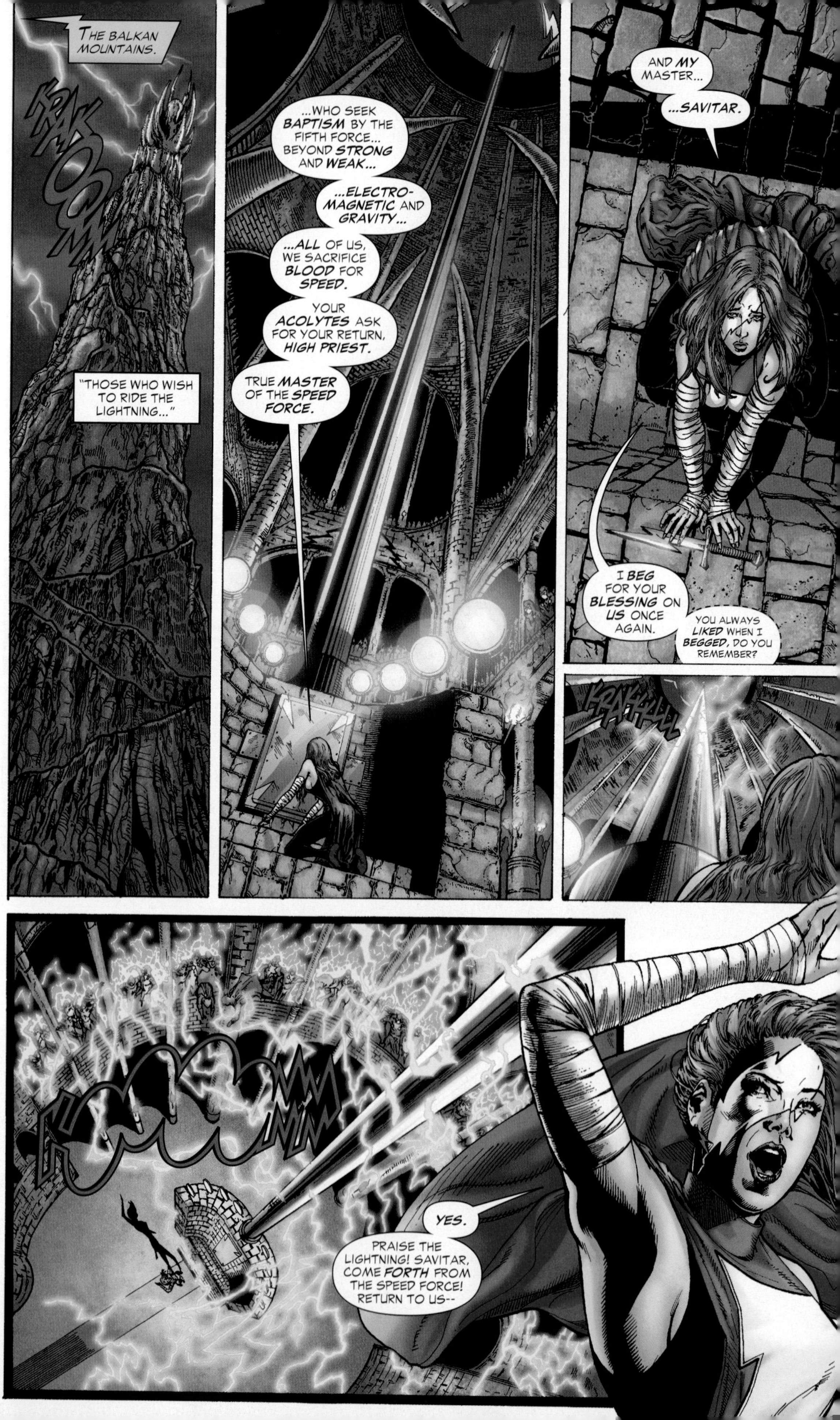
THE BALKAN MOUNTAINS.
"THOSE WHO WISH TO RIDE THE LIGHTNING..."
...WHO SEEK BAPTISM BY THE FIFTH FORCE... BEYOND STRONG AND WEAK...
...ELECTRO-MAGNETIC AND GRAVITY...
...ALL OF US, WE SACRIFICE BLOOD FOR SPEED.
YOUR ACOLYTES ASK FOR YOUR RETURN, HIGH PRIEST.
TRUE MASTER OF THE SPEED FORCE.
AND MY MASTER...
...SAVITAR.
I BEG FOR YOUR BLESSING ON US ONCE AGAIN.
YOU ALWAYS LIKED WHEN I BEGGED, DO YOU REMEMBER?
YES.
PRAISE THE LIGHTNING! SAVITAR, COME FORTH FROM THE SPEED FORCE! RETURN TO US--

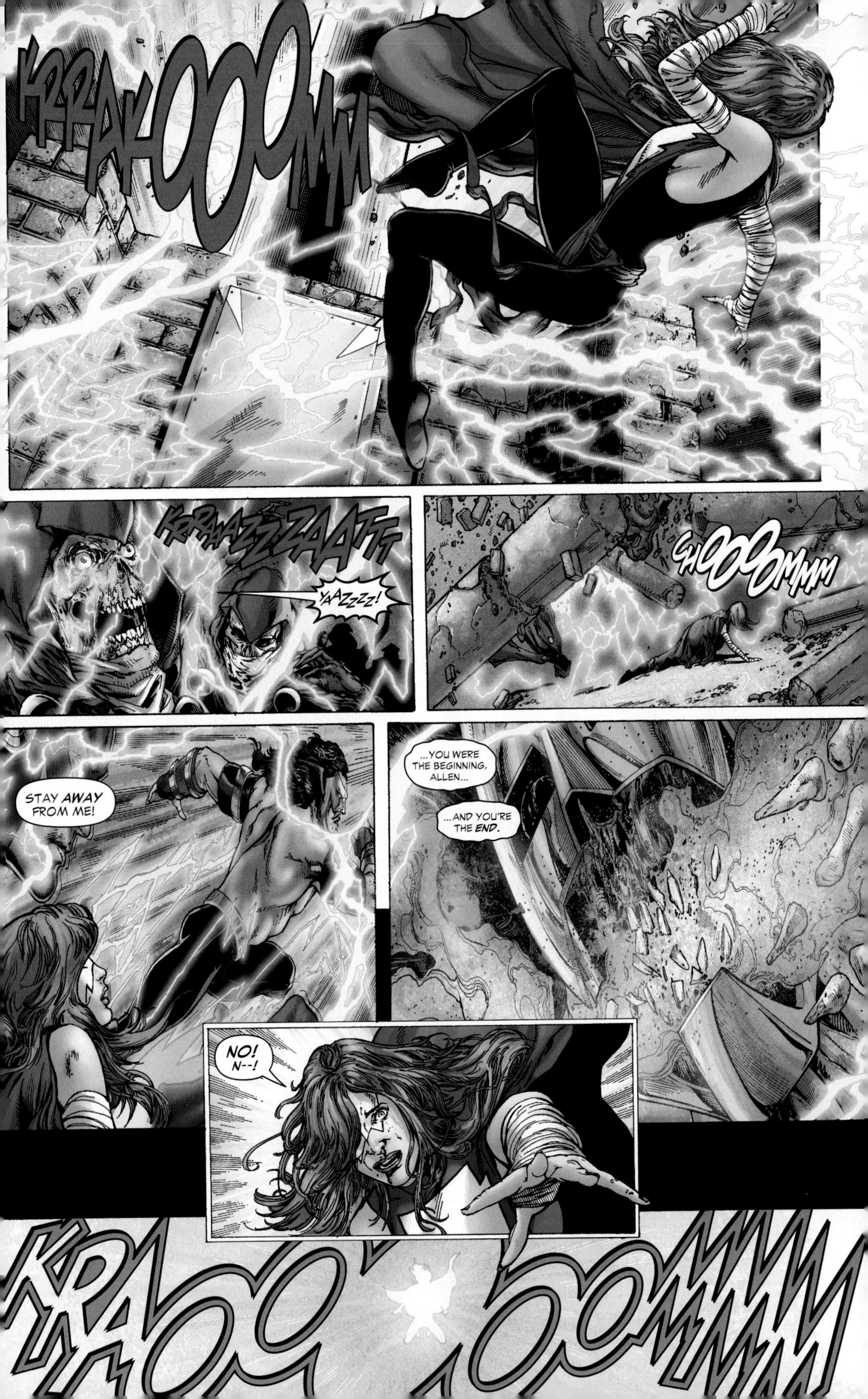
KRRAKOOOMM
KRRAAZZZAATT
YAAZZZZ!
CHOOOOMMM
STAY AWAY FROM ME!
...YOU WERE THE BEGINNING, ALLEN...
...AND YOU'RE THE END.
NO! N--!
KRAOOOOOMMM

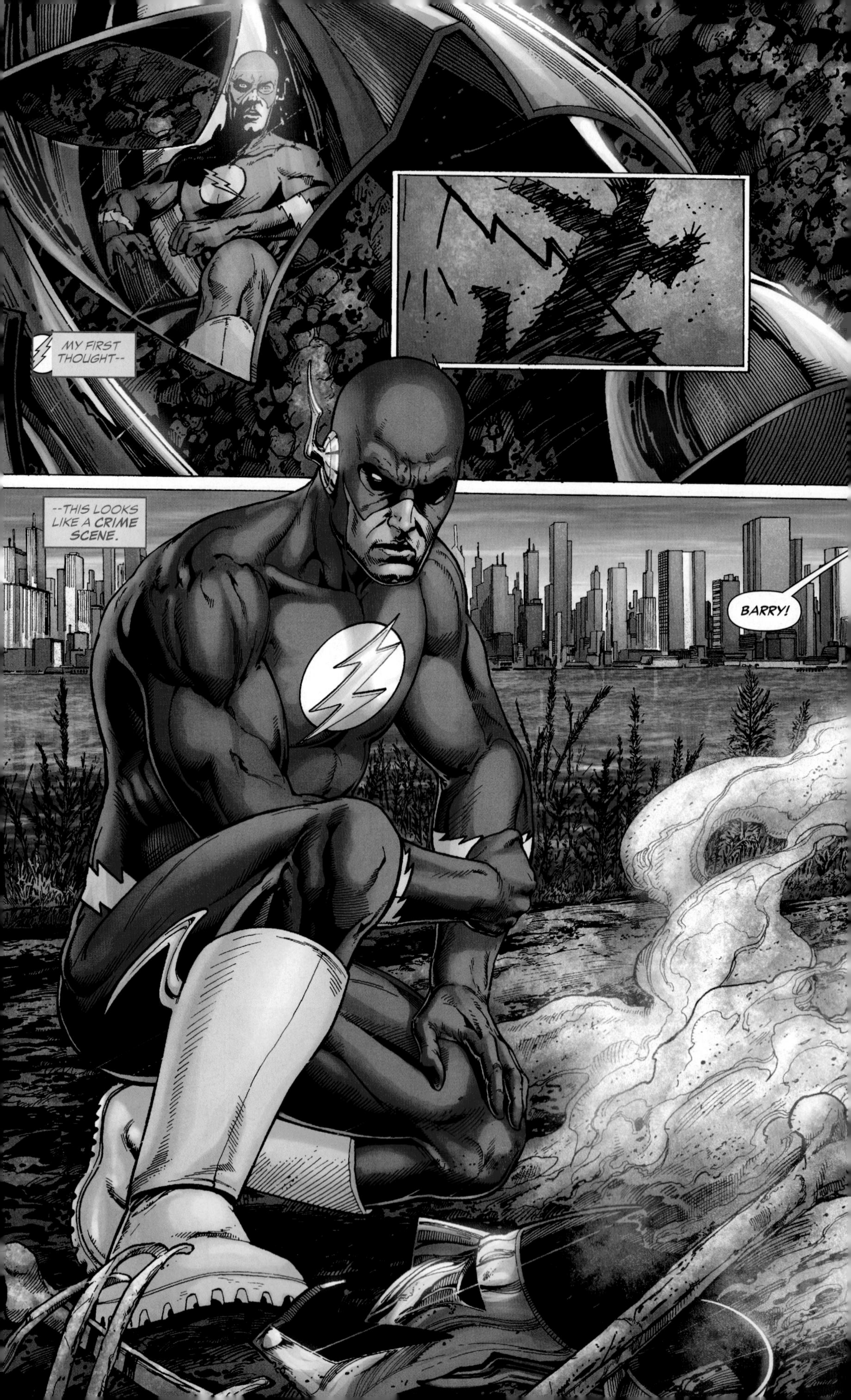
MY FIRST THOUGHT--
--THIS LOOKS LIKE A CRIME SCENE.
BARRY!

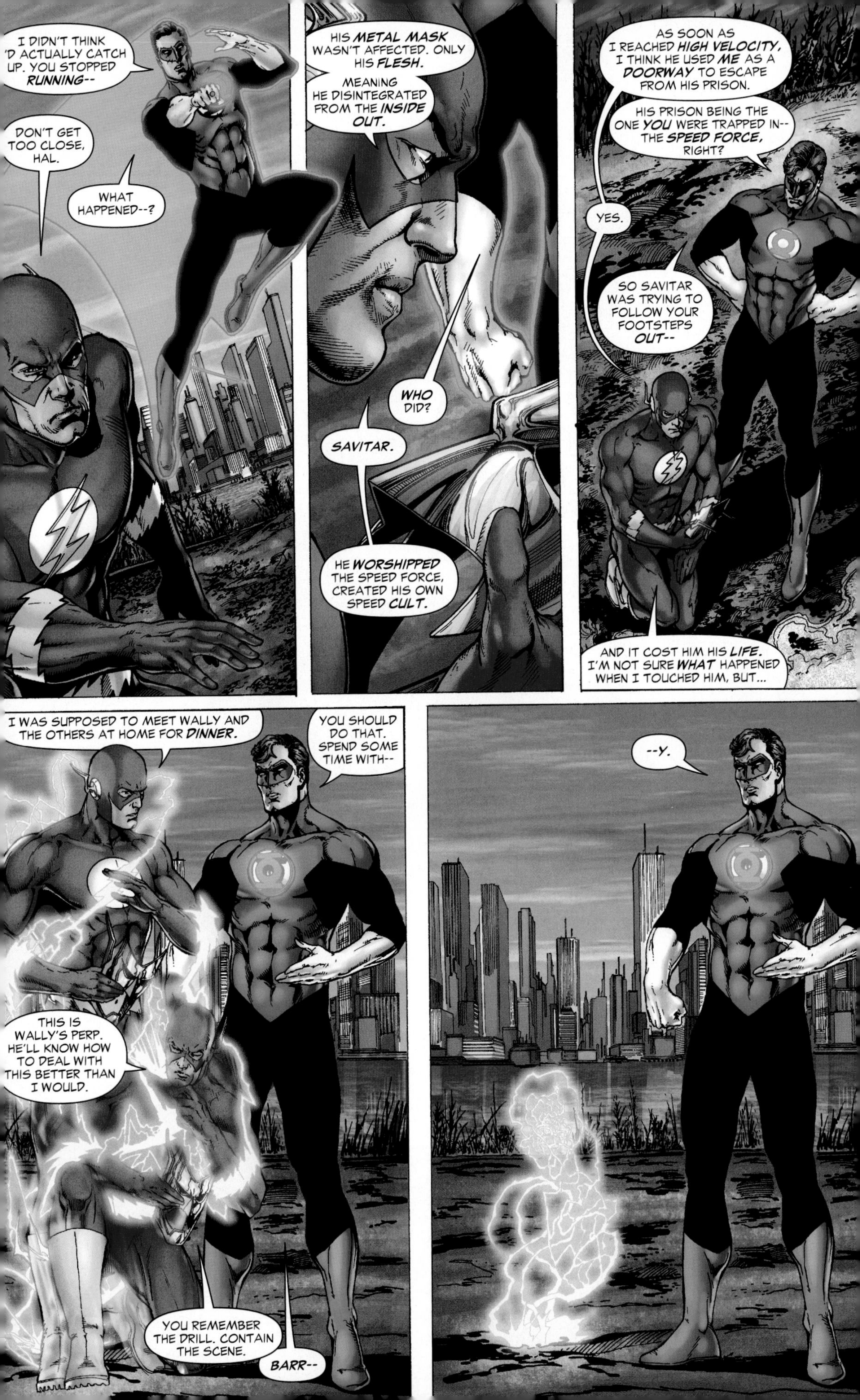
I DIDN'T THINK
'D ACTUALLY CATCH
UP. YOU STOPPED
RUNNING--
DON'T GET
TOO CLOSE,
HAL.
WHAT
HAPPENED--?
HIS METAL MASK
WASN'T AFFECTED. ONLY
HIS FLESH.
MEANING
HE DISINTEGRATED
FROM THE INSIDE
OUT.
WHO
DID?
SAVITAR.
HE WORSHIPPED
THE SPEED FORCE,
CREATED HIS OWN
SPEED CULT.
AS SOON AS
I REACHED HIGH VELOCITY,
I THINK HE USED ME AS A
DOORWAY TO ESCAPE
FROM HIS PRISON.
HIS PRISON BEING THE
ONE YOU WERE TRAPPED IN--
THE SPEED FORCE,
RIGHT?
YES.
SO SAVITAR
WAS TRYING TO
FOLLOW YOUR
FOOTSTEPS
OUT--
AND IT COST HIM HIS LIFE.
I'M NOT SURE WHAT HAPPENED
WHEN I TOUCHED HIM, BUT...
I WAS SUPPOSED TO MEET WALLY AND
THE OTHERS AT HOME FOR DINNER.
YOU SHOULD
DO THAT.
SPEND SOME
TIME WITH--
THIS IS
WALLY'S PERP.
HE'LL KNOW HOW
TO DEAL WITH
THIS BETTER THAN
I WOULD.
YOU REMEMBER
THE DRILL. CONTAIN
THE SCENE.
BARR--
--Y.

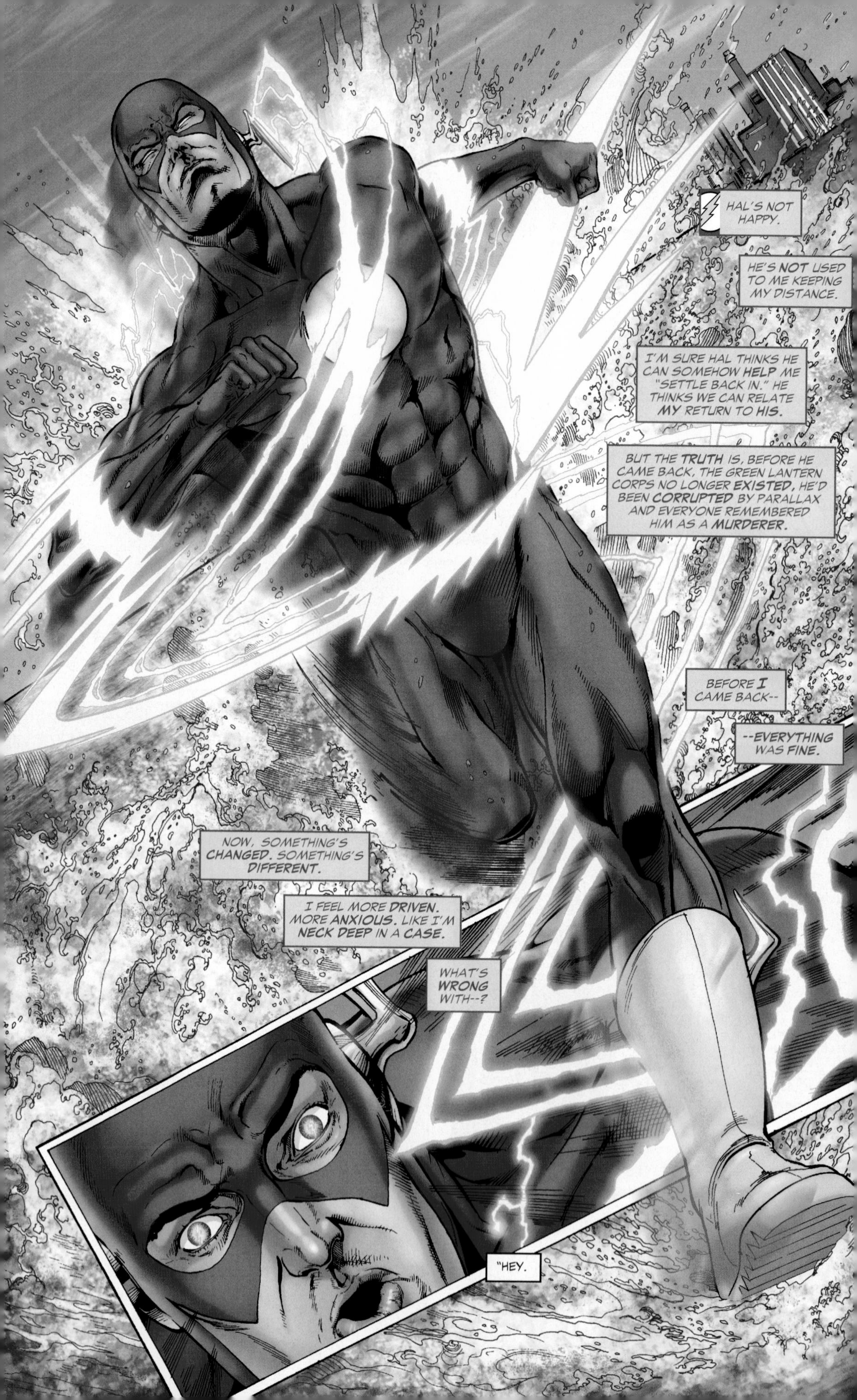
HAL'S NOT HAPPY.
HE'S NOT USED TO ME KEEPING MY DISTANCE.
I'M SURE HAL THINKS HE CAN SOMEHOW HELP ME "SETTLE BACK IN." HE THINKS WE CAN RELATE MY RETURN TO HIS.
BUT THE TRUTH IS, BEFORE HE CAME BACK, THE GREEN LANTERN CORPS NO LONGER EXISTED, HE'D BEEN CORRUPTED BY PARALLAX AND EVERYONE REMEMBERED HIM AS A MURDERER.
BEFORE I CAME BACK--
--EVERYTHING WAS FINE.
NOW, SOMETHING'S CHANGED. SOMETHING'S DIFFERENT.
I FEEL MORE DRIVEN. MORE ANXIOUS. LIKE I'M NECK DEEP IN A CASE.
WHAT'S WRONG WITH--?
"HEY.

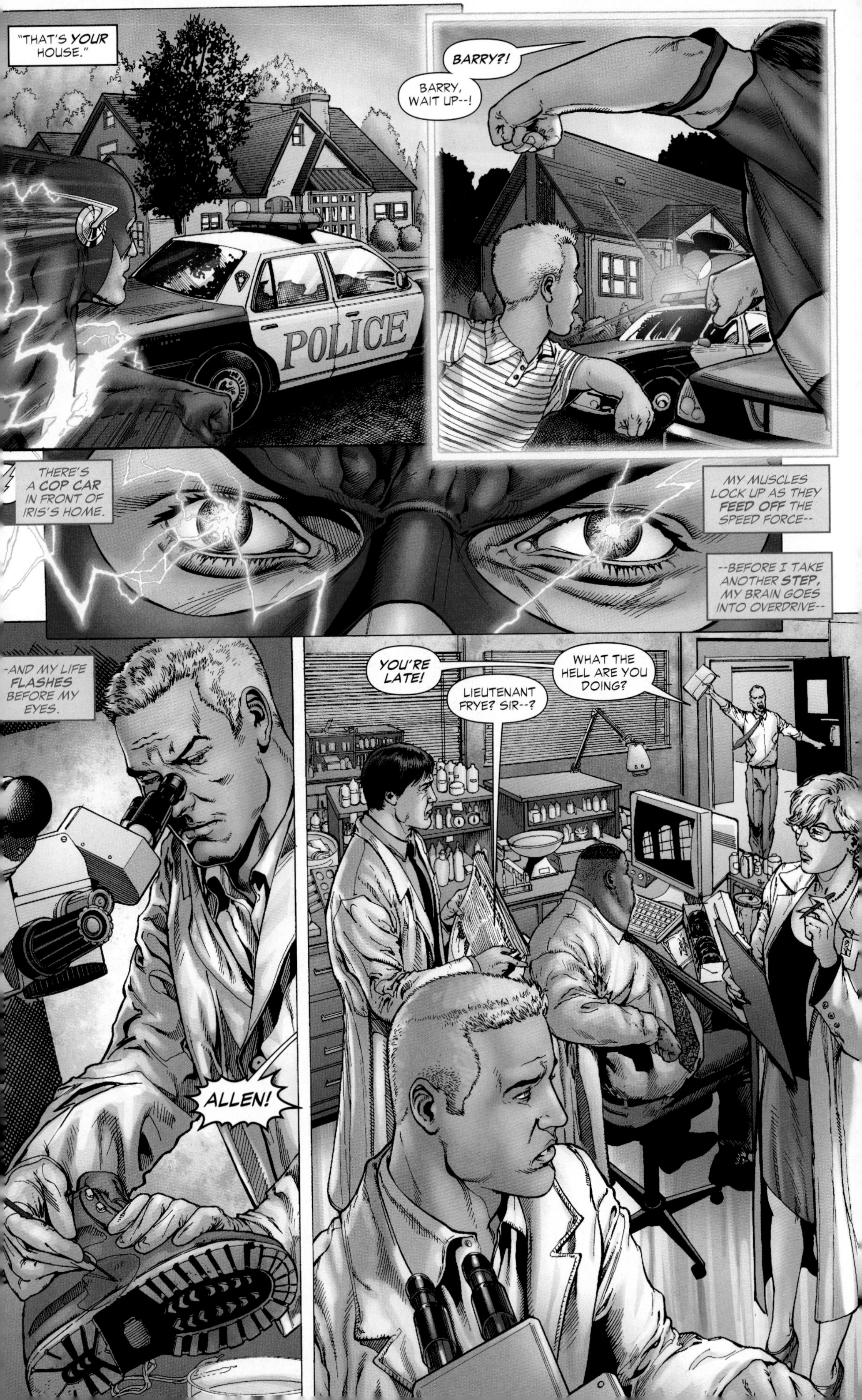
"THAT'S YOUR HOUSE."
BARRY?!
BARRY, WAIT UP--!
POLICE
THERE'S A COP CAR IN FRONT OF IRIS'S HOME.
MY MUSCLES LOCK UP AS THEY FEED OFF THE SPEED FORCE--
--BEFORE I TAKE ANOTHER STEP, MY BRAIN GOES INTO OVERDRIVE--
-AND MY LIFE FLASHES BEFORE MY EYES.
ALLEN!
YOU'RE LATE!
LIEUTENANT FRYE? SIR--?
WHAT THE HELL ARE YOU DOING?

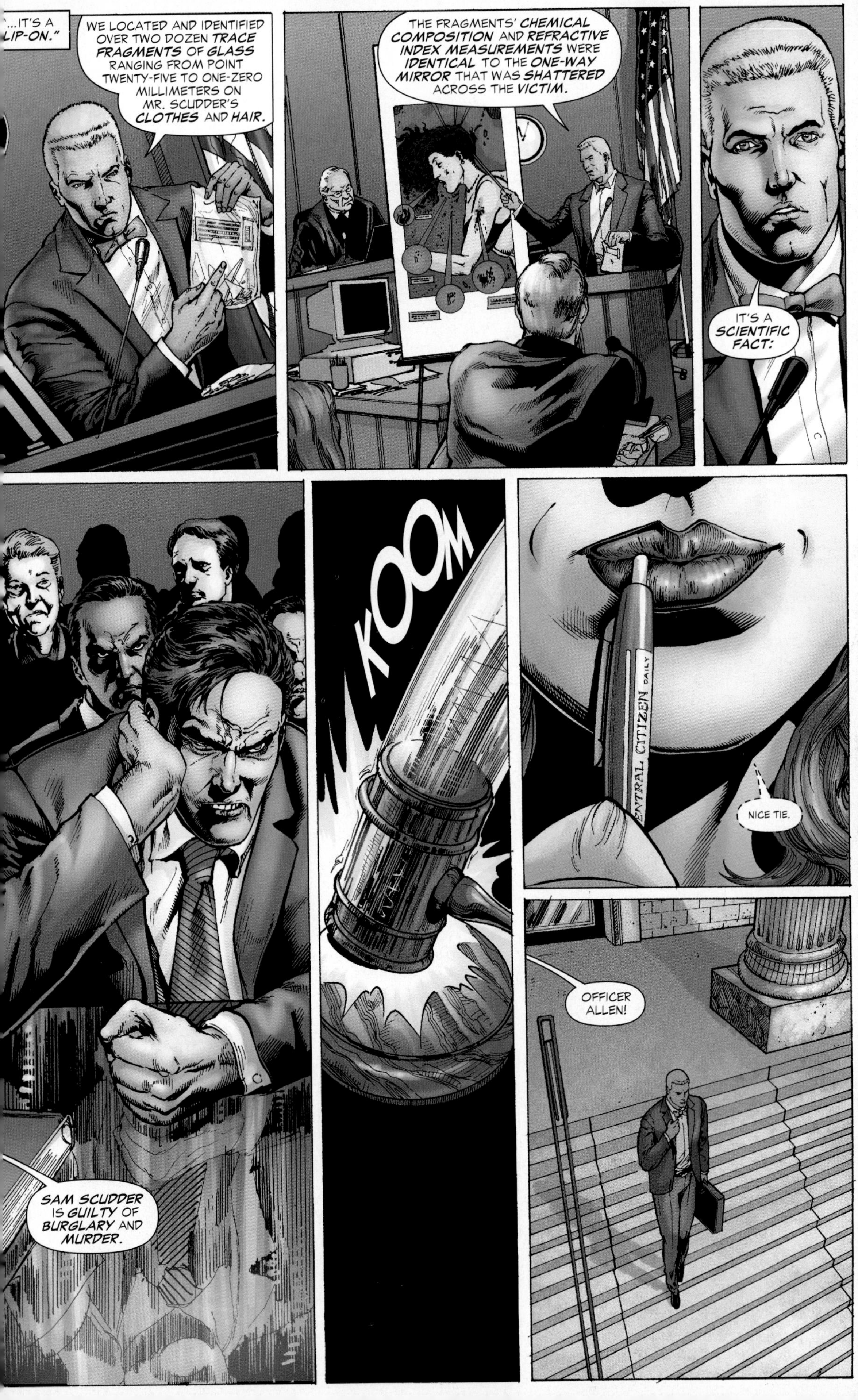
"...IT'S A CLIP-ON."
WE LOCATED AND IDENTIFIED OVER TWO DOZEN TRACE FRAGMENTS OF GLASS RANGING FROM POINT TWENTY-FIVE TO ONE-ZERO MILLIMETERS ON MR. SCUDDER'S CLOTHES AND HAIR.
THE FRAGMENTS' CHEMICAL COMPOSITION AND REFRACTIVE INDEX MEASUREMENTS WERE IDENTICAL TO THE ONE-WAY MIRROR THAT WAS SHATTERED ACROSS THE VICTIM.
IT'S A SCIENTIFIC FACT:
SAM SCUDDER IS GUILTY OF BURGLARY AND MURDER.
KOOM
CENTRAL CITIZEN DAILY
NICE TIE.
OFFICER ALLEN!

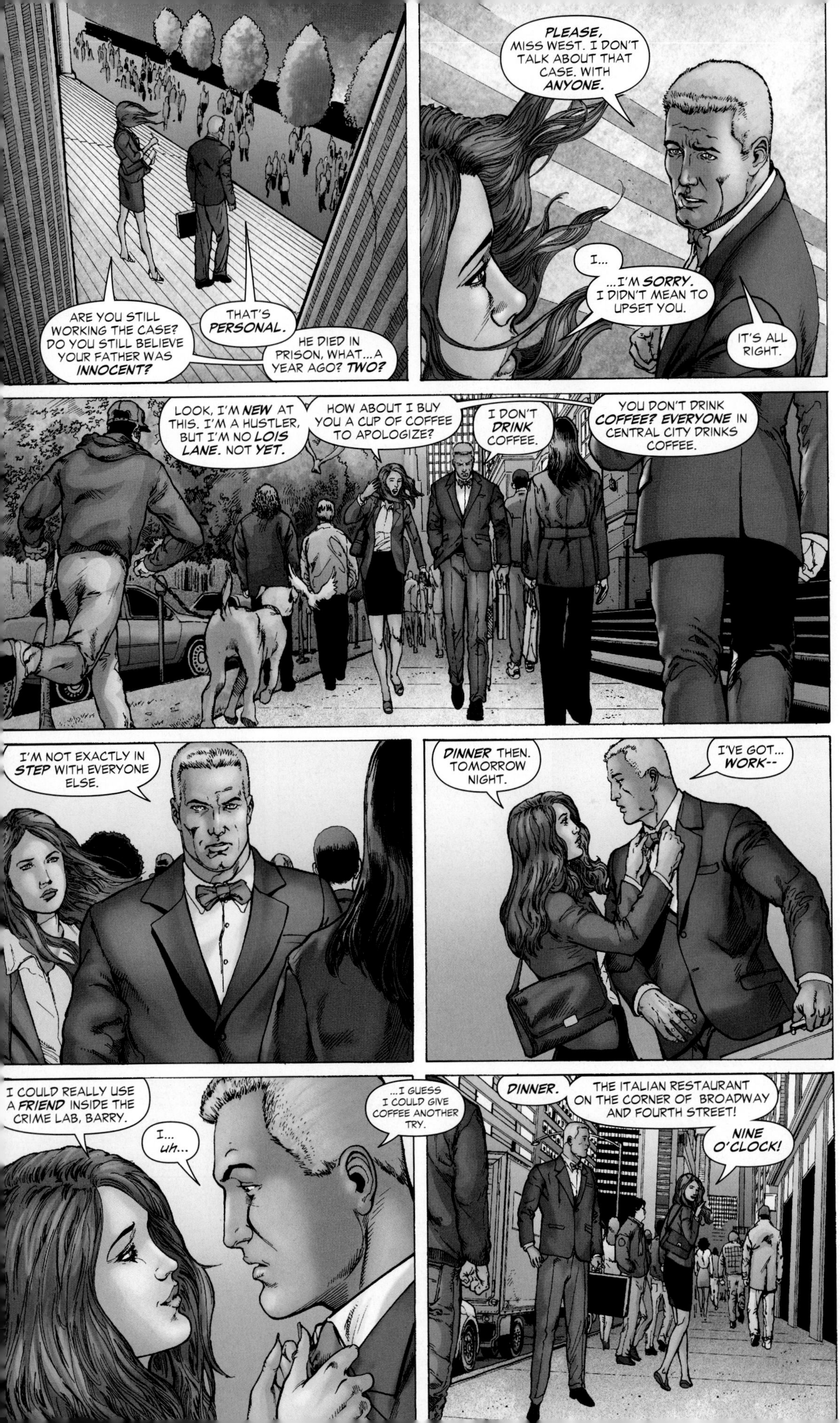

ARE YOU STILL WORKING THE CASE? DO YOU STILL BELIEVE YOUR FATHER WAS INNOCENT?
THAT'S PERSONAL.
HE DIED IN PRISON, WHAT... A YEAR AGO? TWO?
PLEASE, MISS WEST. I DON'T TALK ABOUT THAT CASE. WITH ANYONE.
I...
...I'M SORRY. I DIDN'T MEAN TO UPSET YOU.
IT'S ALL RIGHT.
LOOK, I'M NEW AT THIS. I'M A HUSTLER, BUT I'M NO LOIS LANE. NOT YET.
HOW ABOUT I BUY YOU A CUP OF COFFEE TO APOLOGIZE?
I DON'T DRINK COFFEE.
YOU DON'T DRINK COFFEE? EVERYONE IN CENTRAL CITY DRINKS COFFEE.
I'M NOT EXACTLY IN STEP WITH EVERYONE ELSE.
DINNER THEN. TOMORROW NIGHT.
I'VE GOT... WORK--
I COULD REALLY USE A FRIEND INSIDE THE CRIME LAB, BARRY.
I... uh...
...I GUESS I COULD GIVE COFFEE ANOTHER TRY.
DINNER.
THE ITALIAN RESTAURANT ON THE CORNER OF BROADWAY AND FOURTH STREET!
NINE O'CLOCK!

"AND **DON'T** BE **LATE!**"

SAME THING **EVERY** NIGHT, *huh*, PATTY?

I DON'T THINK I'VE EVER SEEN THE GUY **GO HOME.**

ME EITHER, FORREST.

"WHAT'S HE ALWAYS **WORKING** ON?"

COLD CASES

ALLEN, NORA

"A CASE THAT ONLY **ALLEN** CALLS **COLD.**"

DR. HENRY ALLEN
CONVICTED KILLER
DIES IN PRISON

UNIDENTIFIED

TIK

OH, NO...

...IRIS--

CRAA--

I ALWAYS KEPT IRIS WAITING.

--LATE.

CAPTAIN FRYE?

I WAS ALWAYS--

...THEY COULD USE A CRIME REPORTER LIKE *YOU* AGAIN. THE ONES THE CENTRAL CITY CITIZEN HAVE *HOUNDING* THE STATION NOW ARE ALL *SHOCK,* NO *SUBSTANCE.*

THEY WRITE GRISLY RECAPS OF MURDER *WITHOUT* THE HUMAN STORIES BEHIND THEM.

YOU NEVER GOT *SENSATIONAL* WITH IT, IRIS. YOU ALWAYS MADE IT ABOUT THE *PEOPLE* LEFT BEHIND.

THE *PEOPLE* LEFT BEHIND AND BRINGING THE *GUILTY* TO *JUSTICE* ARE THE ONLY THINGS THAT *MATTER* IN A HOMICIDE.

EVERYONE IN THE WORLD THINKS BARRY ALLEN IS DEAD.

WHY DOESN'T FRYE?

I APPRECIATE YOUR BEING *DISCREET* ABOUT BARRY'S RETURN, CAPTAIN FRYE.

YOUR HUSBAND WAS ONE OF THE FINEST POLICE OFFICERS I'VE EVER KNOWN, IRIS. WHEN I RECEIVED THE CALL FROM THE F.B.I., I WAS THRILLED TO KNOW HE WAS *ALIVE.*

IT'S NOT OFTEN SOMEONE IN *WITNESS PROTECTION* GETS THEIR LIFE BACK.

WITNESS PROTECTION?

WHERE HAS ALLEN BEEN *HIDING* ALL THESE YEARS *ANYWAY?*

SOMEWHERE *WARM.*

"IT STARTED WITH JAY."

NEW YORK.

I'M *FINE*, JOAN. JUST A LITTLE *WINDED*.

THE BROWNSTONE OF THE JUSTICE SOCIETY OF AMERICA.

"APPARENTLY, HE EXPERIENCED SOME KIND OF '*SPEED SEIZURE.*'

"HE COLLAPSED.

"LIBERTY BELLE SUFFERED SOMETHING SIMILAR, BUT TO A MUCH *LESSER* EXTENT. SHE'S NO LONGER AS CONNECTED TO THE SPEED FORCE LIKE HER FATHER WAS, BUT S STILL HAS SOME KIND OF RESIDUAL TIE.

"BART'S A *DIFFERENT STORY.* HIS SEIZURE WAS LONGER THAN JAY'S, AND MORE PAINFUL."

SAN FRANCISCO.

TEEN TITANS TOWER.

I WANT TO TALK TO WALLY.

THEY DON'T WANT YOU *RUNNING* UNTIL WE FINISH THESE TESTS.

CAN'T YOU DO IT ANY *FASTER?*

NO, BART.

AW, MAN.

"THE SAME KIND OF *SPEED FORCE SURGE* STRUCK ME AND THE KIDS."

THANKS, BUT I DON'T FEEL LIKE ICE CREAM.

NEW YORK.

TITANS TOWER.

A VANILLA FOR IREY AND A CHOCOLATE FOR JAI.

BUT YOU *LOVE* ICE CREAM.

"WE'RE RUNNING TESTS--"

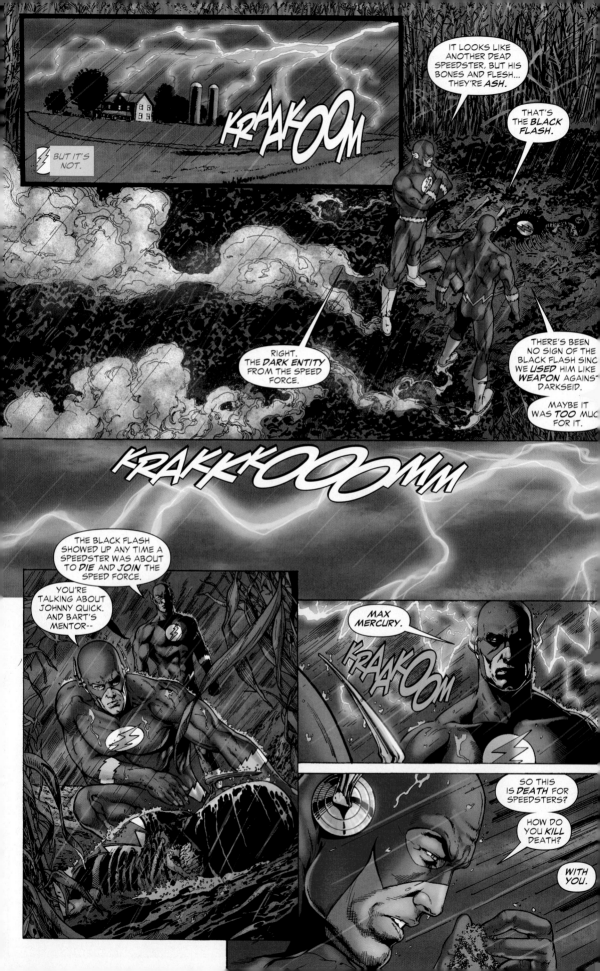

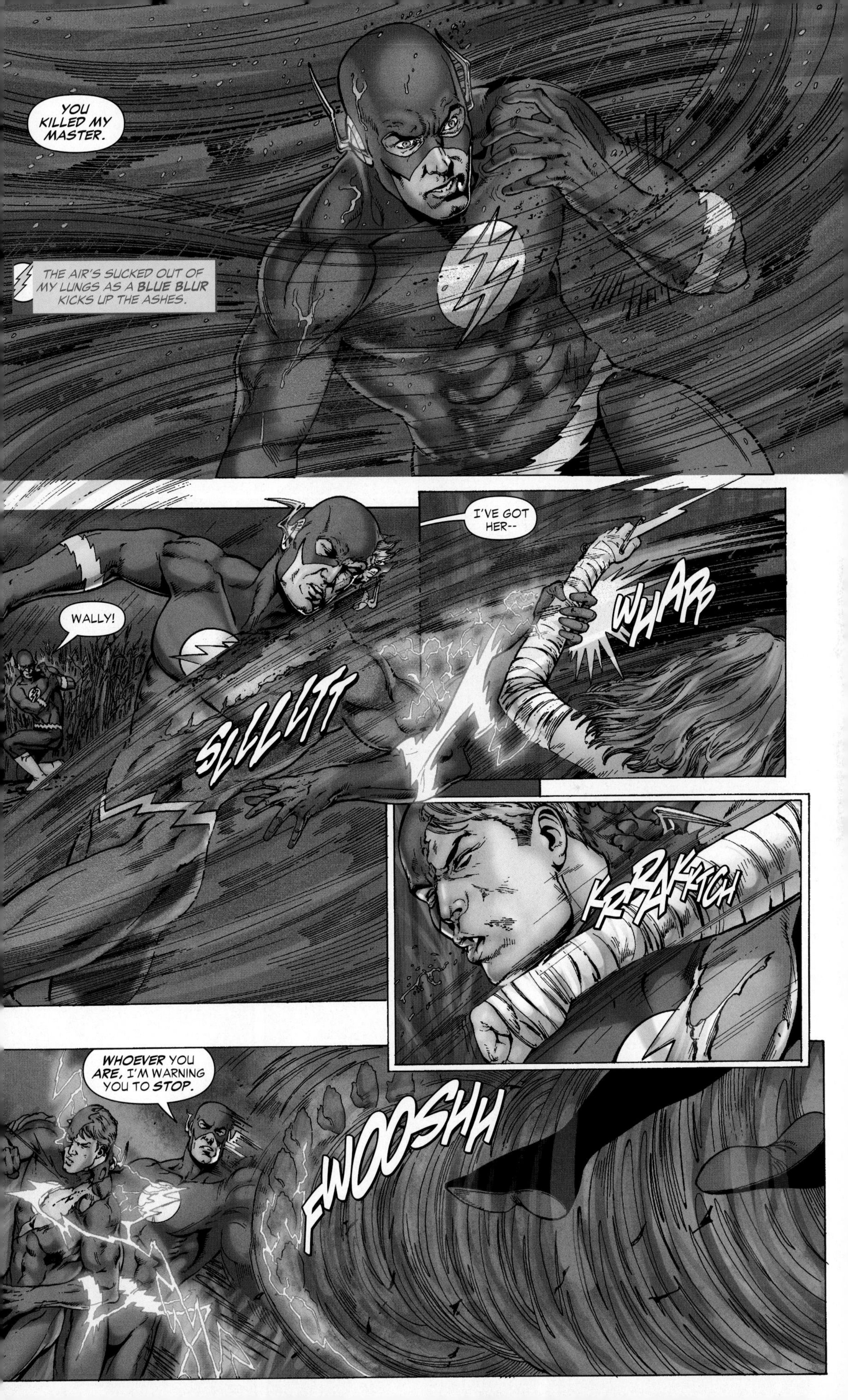

YOU KILLED MY MASTER.
THE AIR'S SUCKED OUT OF MY LUNGS AS A BLUE BLUR KICKS UP THE ASHES.
I'VE GOT HER--
WALLY!
WHAPP
SLLLLTT
KRRAKKTCH
WHOEVER YOU ARE, I'M WARNING YOU TO STOP.
FWOOSHH

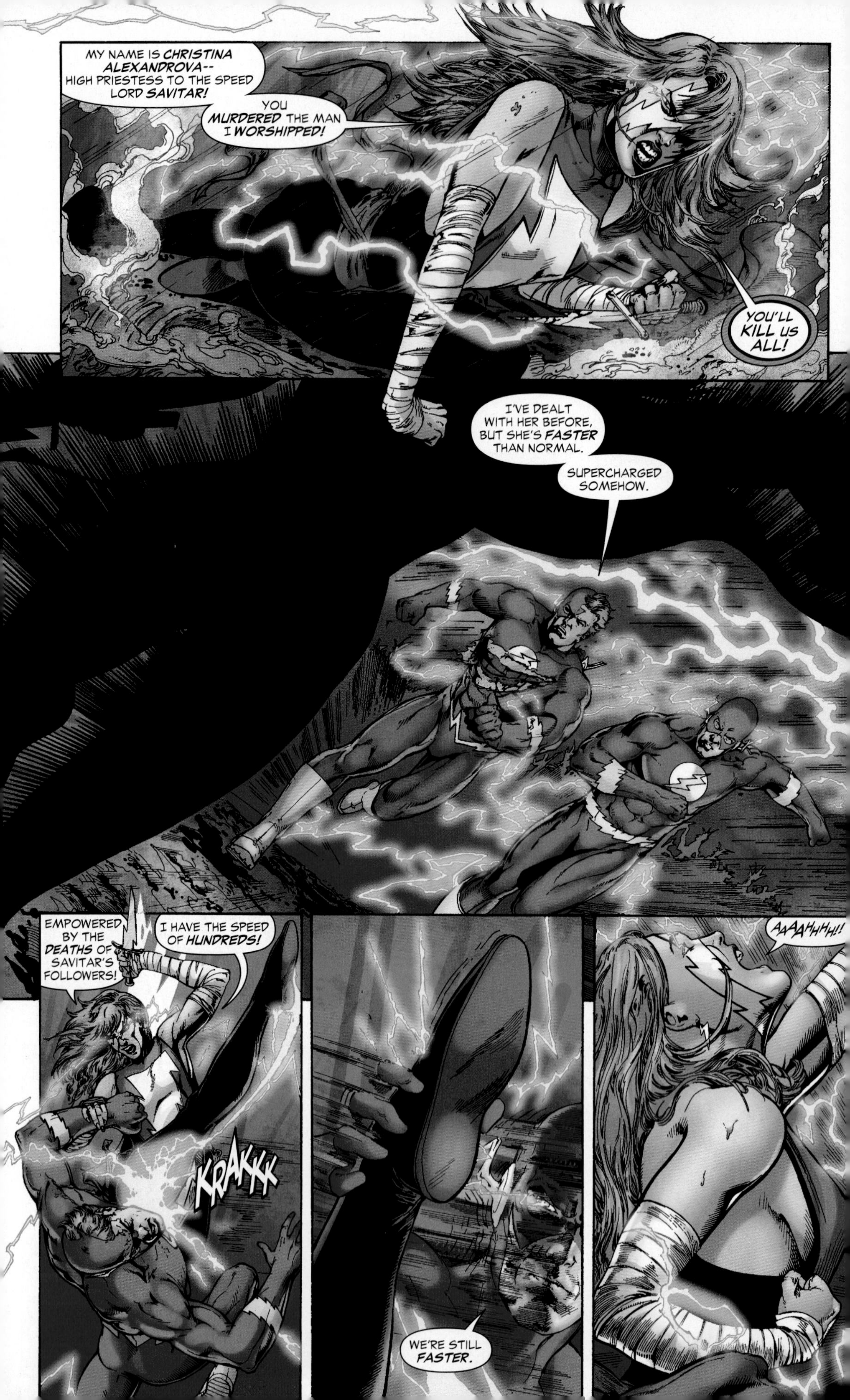
MY NAME IS CHRISTINA ALEXANDROVA-- HIGH PRIESTESS TO THE SPEED LORD SAVITAR!
YOU MURDERED THE MAN I WORSHIPPED!
YOU'LL KILL US ALL!
I'VE DEALT WITH HER BEFORE, BUT SHE'S FASTER THAN NORMAL.
SUPERCHARGED SOMEHOW.
EMPOWERED BY THE DEATHS OF SAVITAR'S FOLLOWERS!
I HAVE THE SPEED OF HUNDREDS!
KRAKKK
WE'RE STILL FASTER.
AAAAHHHH!!

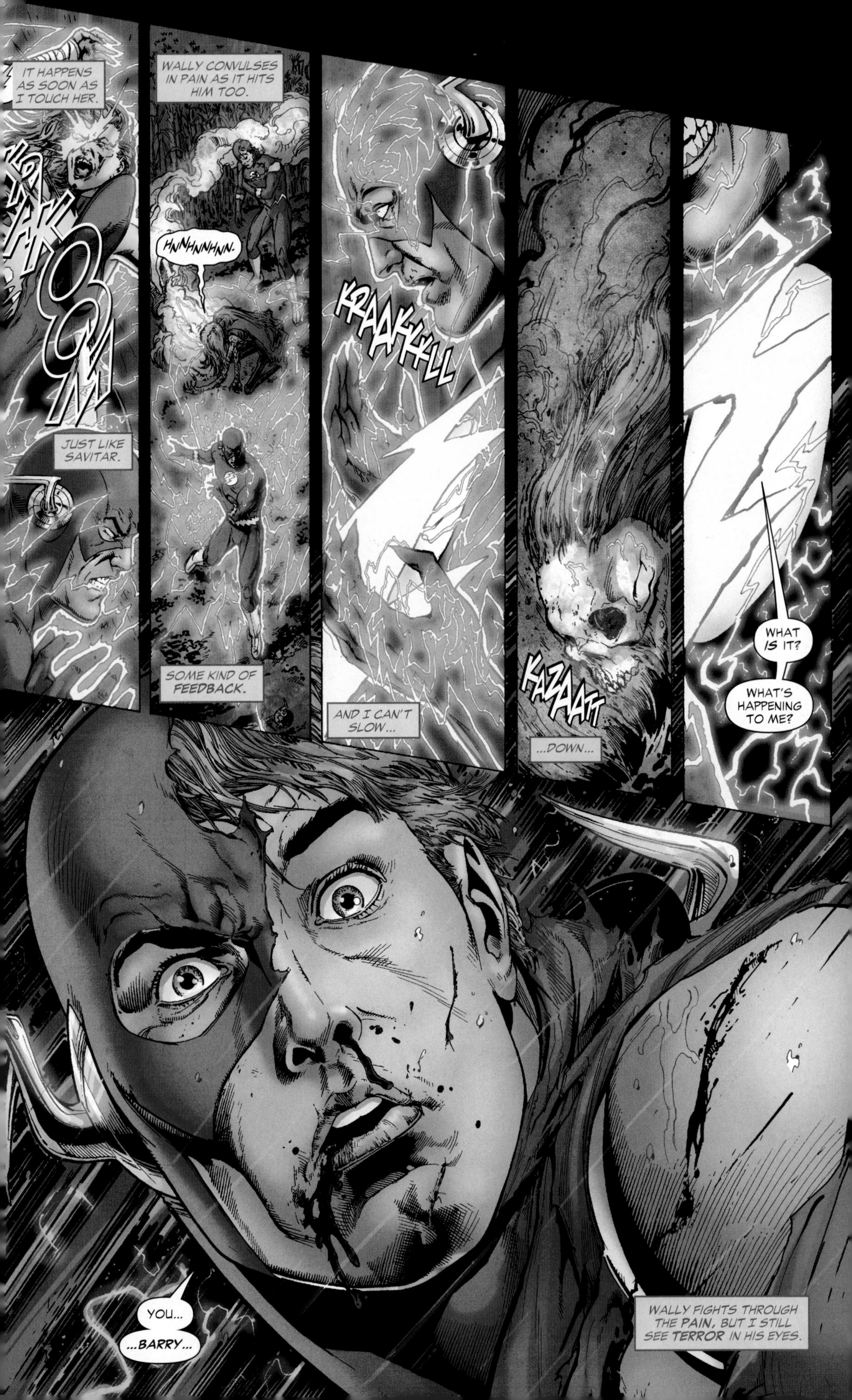
IT HAPPENS AS SOON AS I TOUCH HER.
KKAKOOM
JUST LIKE SAVITAR.
WALLY CONVULSES IN PAIN AS IT HITS HIM TOO.
HNNHNNHNN.
SOME KIND OF FEEDBACK.
KRAAKKLL
AND I CAN'T SLOW...
KAZAAKK
...DOWN...
WHAT IS IT?
WHAT'S HAPPENING TO ME?
YOU...
...BARRY...
WALLY FIGHTS THROUGH THE PAIN, BUT I STILL SEE TERROR IN HIS EYES.

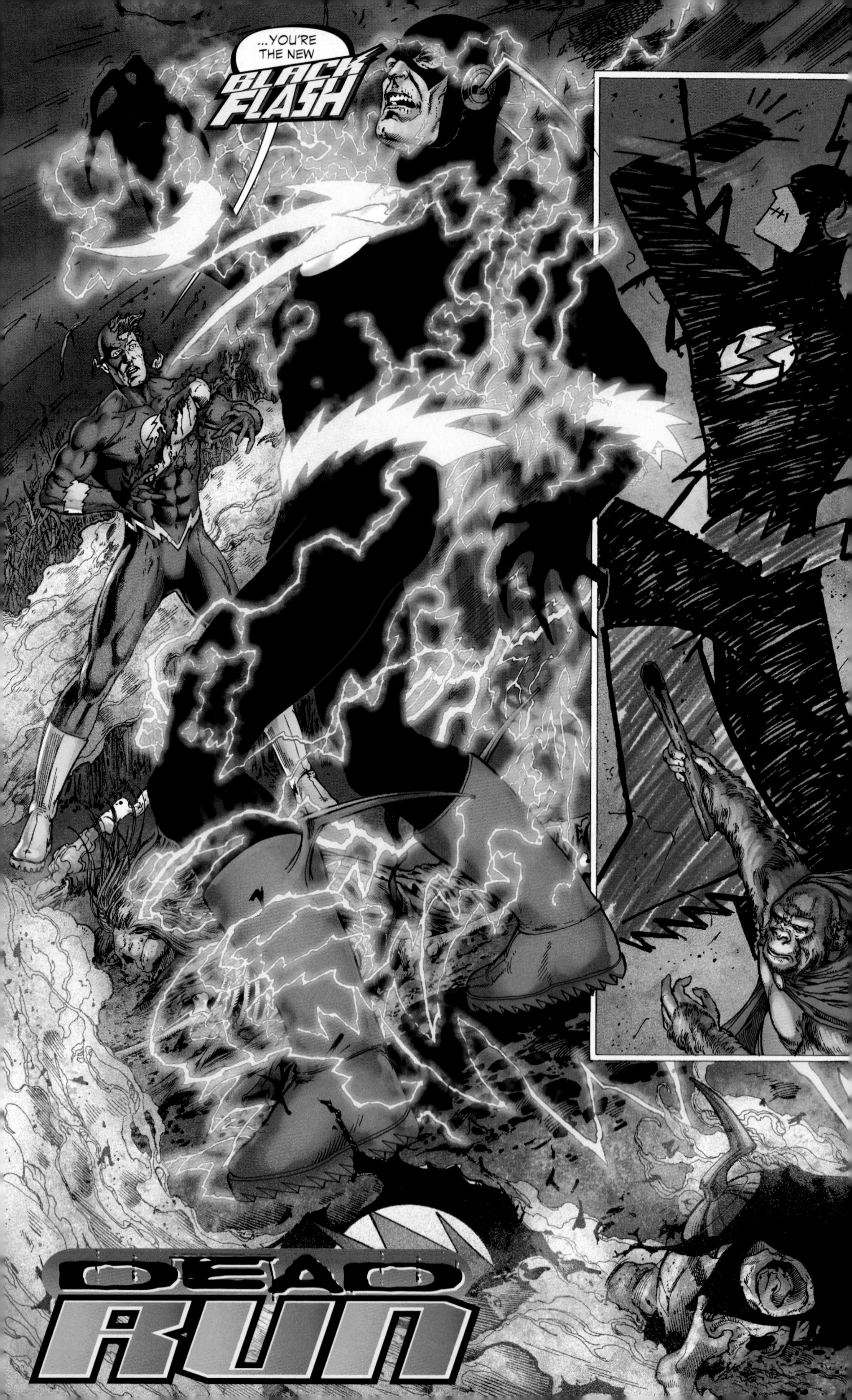

...YOU'RE THE NEW BLACK FLASH
DEAD RUN

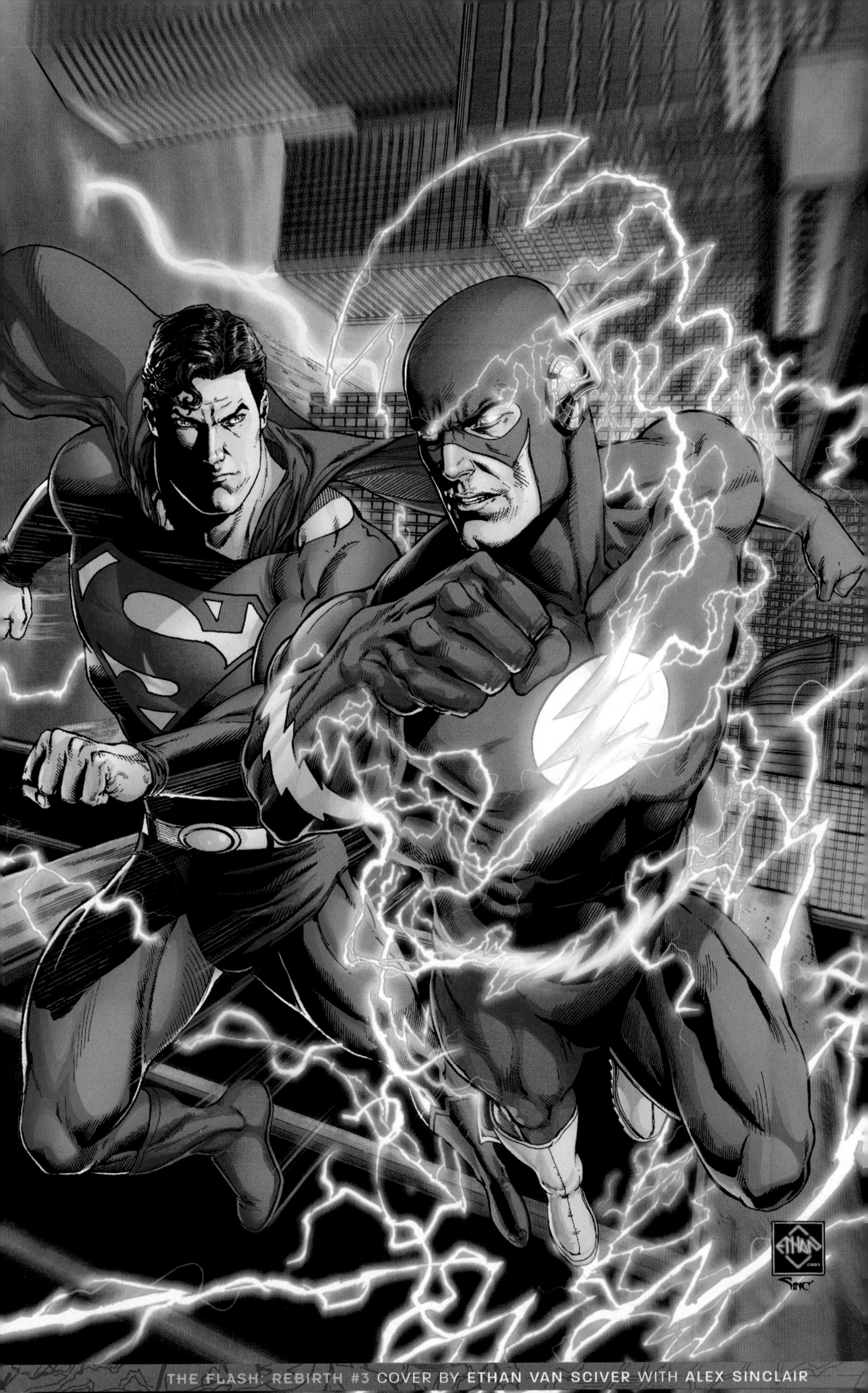

THE FLASH: REBIRTH #3 COVER BY ETHAN VAN SCIVER WITH ALEX SINCLAIR

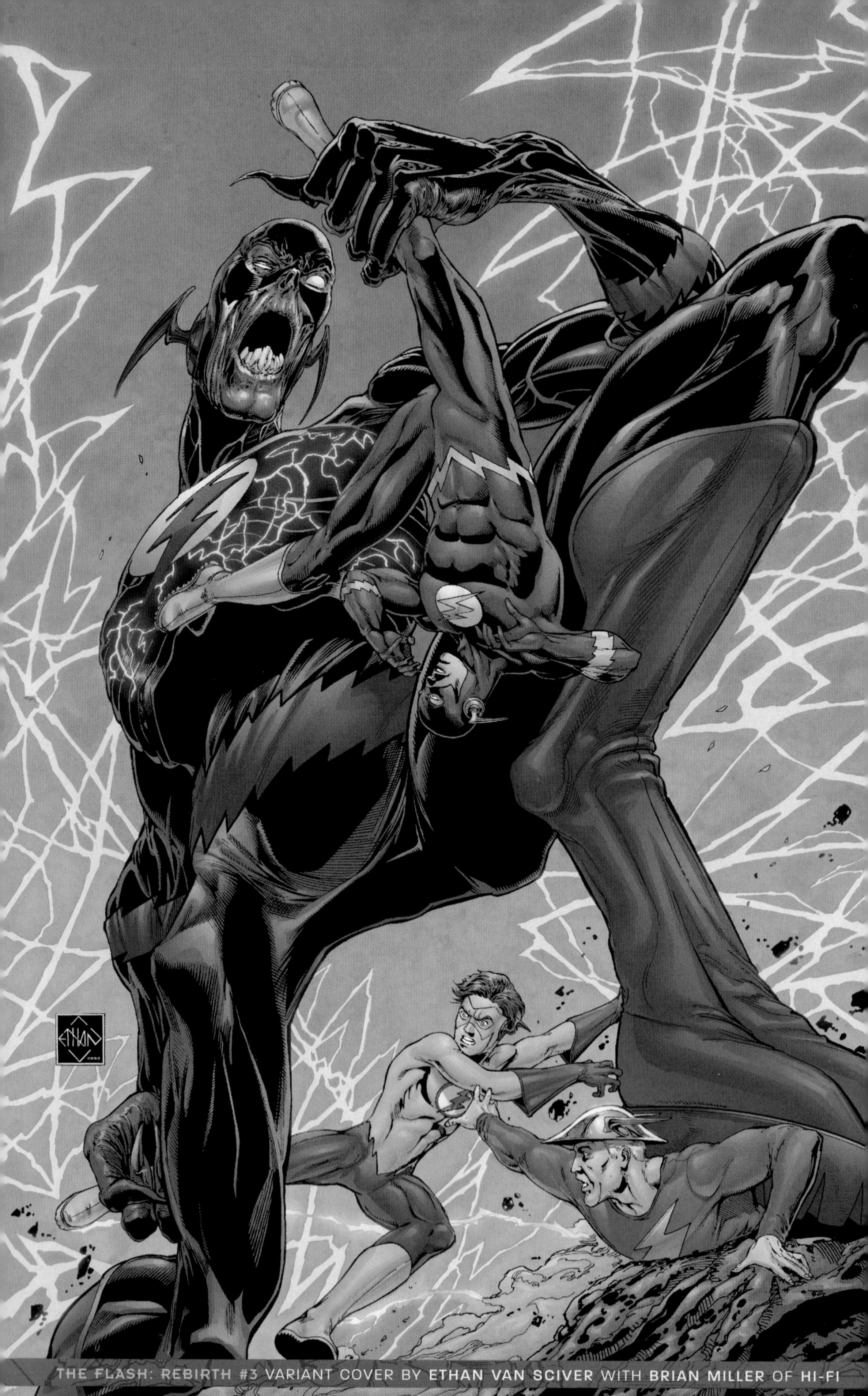

THE FLASH: REBIRTH #3 VARIANT COVER BY **ETHAN VAN SCIVER** WITH **BRIAN MILLER** OF **HI-FI**

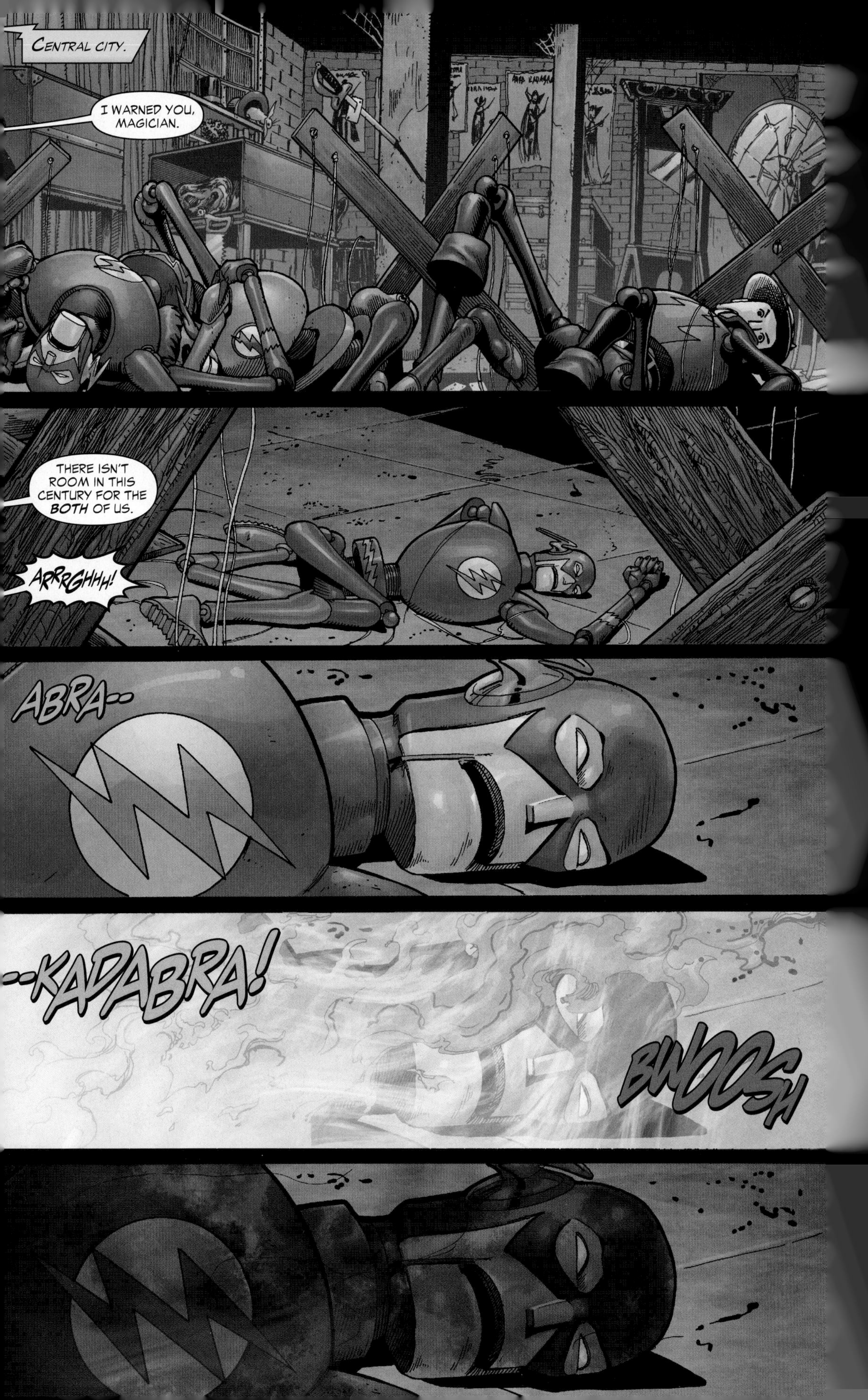
CENTRAL CITY.
I WARNED YOU, MAGICIAN.
THERE ISN'T ROOM IN THIS CENTURY FOR THE BOTH OF US.
ARRRGHHH!
ABRA--
--KADABRA!
BWOOSH

NEW YORK CITY.

HEADQUARTERS OF THE JUSTICE SOCIETY OF AMERICA.

JESSE?

HON? DR. MID-NITE SAID YOU SHOULDN'T BE ON YOUR FEET. YOU MIGHT RISK TRIGGERING YOUR TIE TO THE SPEED FORCE AGAIN.

WHAT ARE YOU DOING OUT HERE?

WHY'D THEY PUT THEM TOGETHER LIKE THIS, RICK?

MY PARENTS SEPARATED WHEN I WAS A KID.

JOHNNY QUICK AND LIBERTY BELLE WERE THE QUINTESSENTIAL COUPLE OF THE ALL-STAR SQUADRON, JESS.

PEOPLE LIKE TO REMEMBER THINGS IN THEIR BEST LIGHT.

IF BECOMING LIBERTY BELLE BROUGHT YOU CLOSER TO YOUR MOTHER, YOUR DAD WOULD'VE THOUGHT IT WAS A GOOD THING.

I HOPE SO.

WHAT WOULD DAD THINK IF HE CAME BACK?

I TRIED TO FILL HIS BOOTS BY BECOMING JESSE QUICK. BUT WHEN MY CONNECTION TO THE SPEED FORCE WEAKENED, I LET IT SLIP AWAY AND I RAN TOWARDS MY MOTHER.

EVEN THOUGH IT WAS DAD WHO WAS ALWAYS THERE FOR ME. WHO ALWAYS SUPPORTED ME.

KRAKLL

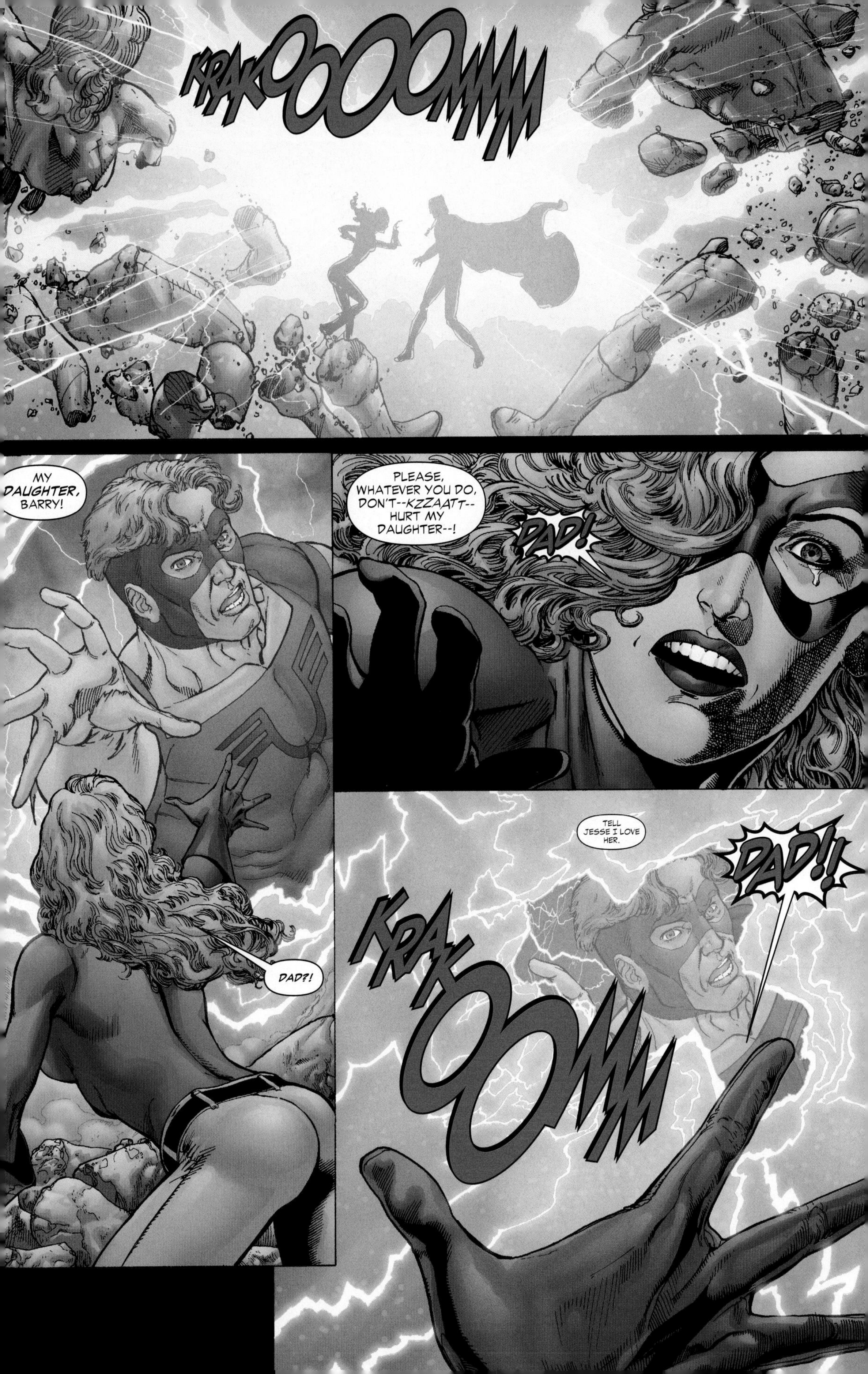
KRAKOOOOOMMMM
MY DAUGHTER, BARRY!
DAD?!
PLEASE, WHATEVER YOU DO, DON'T--KZZAATT--HURT MY DAUGHTER--!
DAD!
TELL JESSE I LOVE HER.
DAD!!
KRAKOOMMM

FALLVILLE, IOWA.

I RECOGNIZE SOME OF THEM AS THEY ARRIVE. A LOT OF THE OTHERS ARE ENTIRELY NEW TO ME.

KRAKOOOMMM

BUT THEY'RE ALL HERE TO DO THE SAME THING.

WE'RE GOING TO *HELP* YOU, BARRY.

KA-ZAAATT

PLEASE, WALLY. STAY AWAY FROM ME.

THEY WANT TO BRING A DEAD MAN BACK TO LIFE.

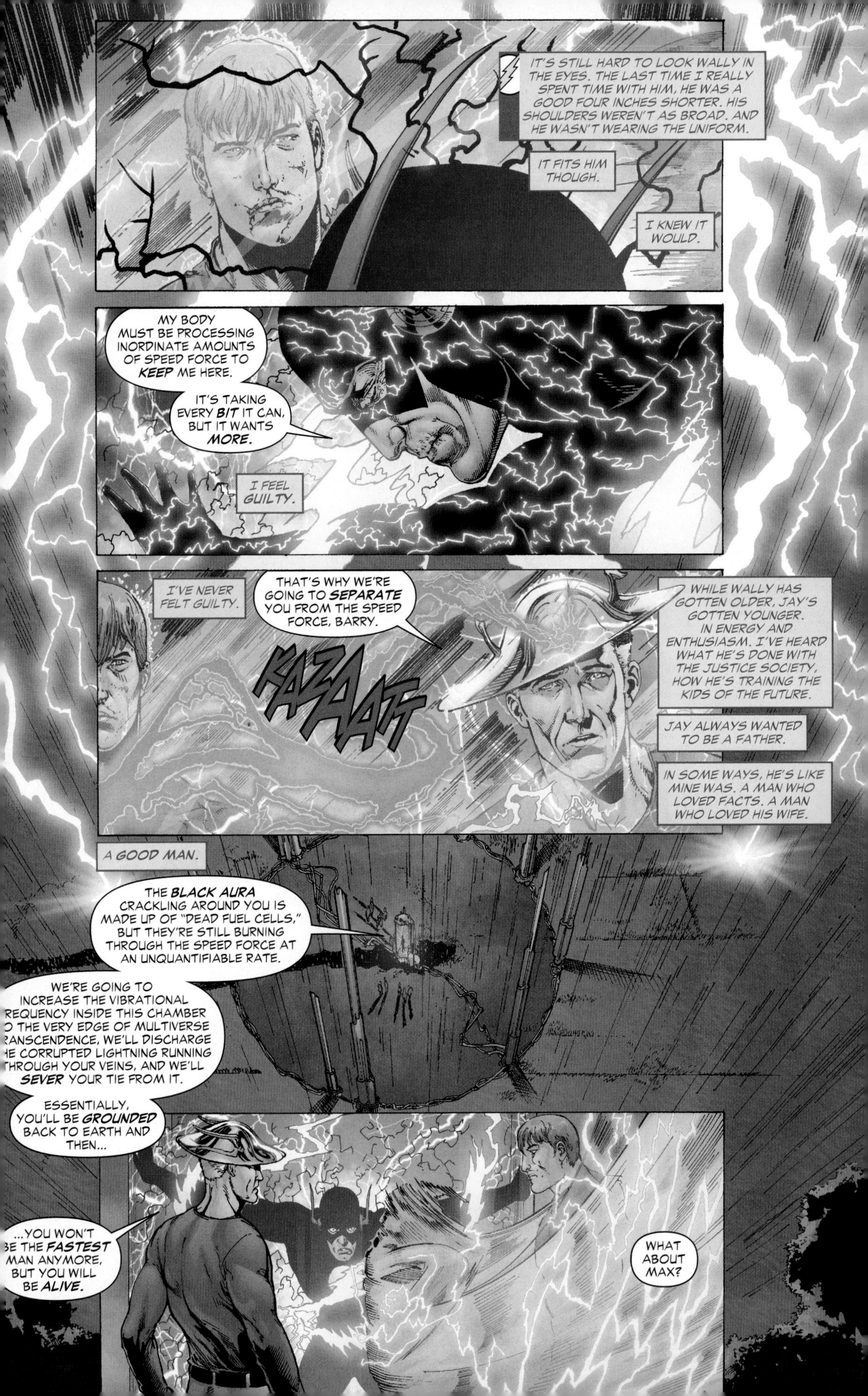

IT'S STILL HARD TO LOOK WALLY IN THE EYES. THE LAST TIME I REALLY SPENT TIME WITH HIM, HE WAS A GOOD FOUR INCHES SHORTER. HIS SHOULDERS WEREN'T AS BROAD. AND HE WASN'T WEARING THE UNIFORM.
IT FITS HIM THOUGH.
I KNEW IT WOULD.
MY BODY MUST BE PROCESSING INORDINATE AMOUNTS OF SPEED FORCE TO KEEP ME HERE.
IT'S TAKING EVERY BIT IT CAN, BUT IT WANTS MORE.
I FEEL GUILTY.
I'VE NEVER FELT GUILTY.
THAT'S WHY WE'RE GOING TO SEPARATE YOU FROM THE SPEED FORCE, BARRY.
KAZAATT
WHILE WALLY HAS GOTTEN OLDER, JAY'S GOTTEN YOUNGER. IN ENERGY AND ENTHUSIASM. I'VE HEARD WHAT HE'S DONE WITH THE JUSTICE SOCIETY, HOW HE'S TRAINING THE KIDS OF THE FUTURE.
JAY ALWAYS WANTED TO BE A FATHER.
IN SOME WAYS, HE'S LIKE MINE WAS. A MAN WHO LOVED FACTS. A MAN WHO LOVED HIS WIFE.
A GOOD MAN.
THE BLACK AURA CRACKLING AROUND YOU IS MADE UP OF "DEAD FUEL CELLS," BUT THEY'RE STILL BURNING THROUGH THE SPEED FORCE AT AN UNQUANTIFIABLE RATE.
WE'RE GOING TO INCREASE THE VIBRATIONAL REQUENCY INSIDE THIS CHAMBER O THE VERY EDGE OF MULTIVERSE RANSCENDENCE, WE'LL DISCHARGE HE CORRUPTED LIGHTNING RUNNING THROUGH YOUR VEINS, AND WE'LL SEVER YOUR TIE FROM IT.
ESSENTIALLY, YOU'LL BE GROUNDED BACK TO EARTH AND THEN...
...YOU WON'T BE THE FASTEST MAN ANYMORE, BUT YOU WILL BE ALIVE.
WHAT ABOUT MAX?

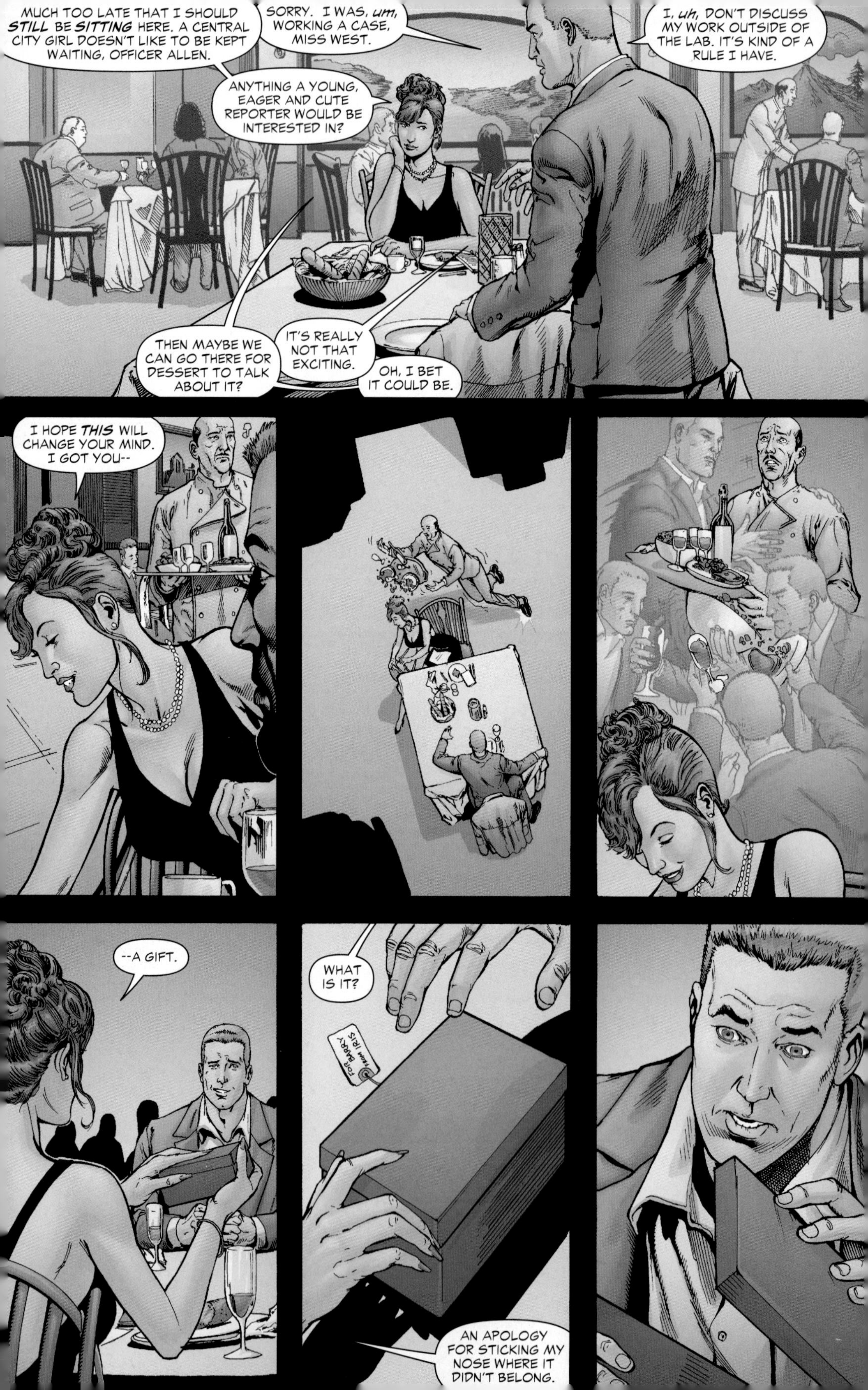
MUCH TOO LATE THAT I SHOULD STILL BE SITTING HERE. A CENTRAL CITY GIRL DOESN'T LIKE TO BE KEPT WAITING, OFFICER ALLEN.
SORRY. I WAS, UM, WORKING A CASE, MISS WEST.
ANYTHING A YOUNG, EAGER AND CUTE REPORTER WOULD BE INTERESTED IN?
I, UH, DON'T DISCUSS MY WORK OUTSIDE OF THE LAB. IT'S KIND OF A RULE I HAVE.
THEN MAYBE WE CAN GO THERE FOR DESSERT TO TALK ABOUT IT?
IT'S REALLY NOT THAT EXCITING.
OH, I BET IT COULD BE.
I HOPE THIS WILL CHANGE YOUR MIND. I GOT YOU--
--A GIFT.
WHAT IS IT?
FOR BARRY FROM IRIS
AN APOLOGY FOR STICKING MY NOSE WHERE IT DIDN'T BELONG.

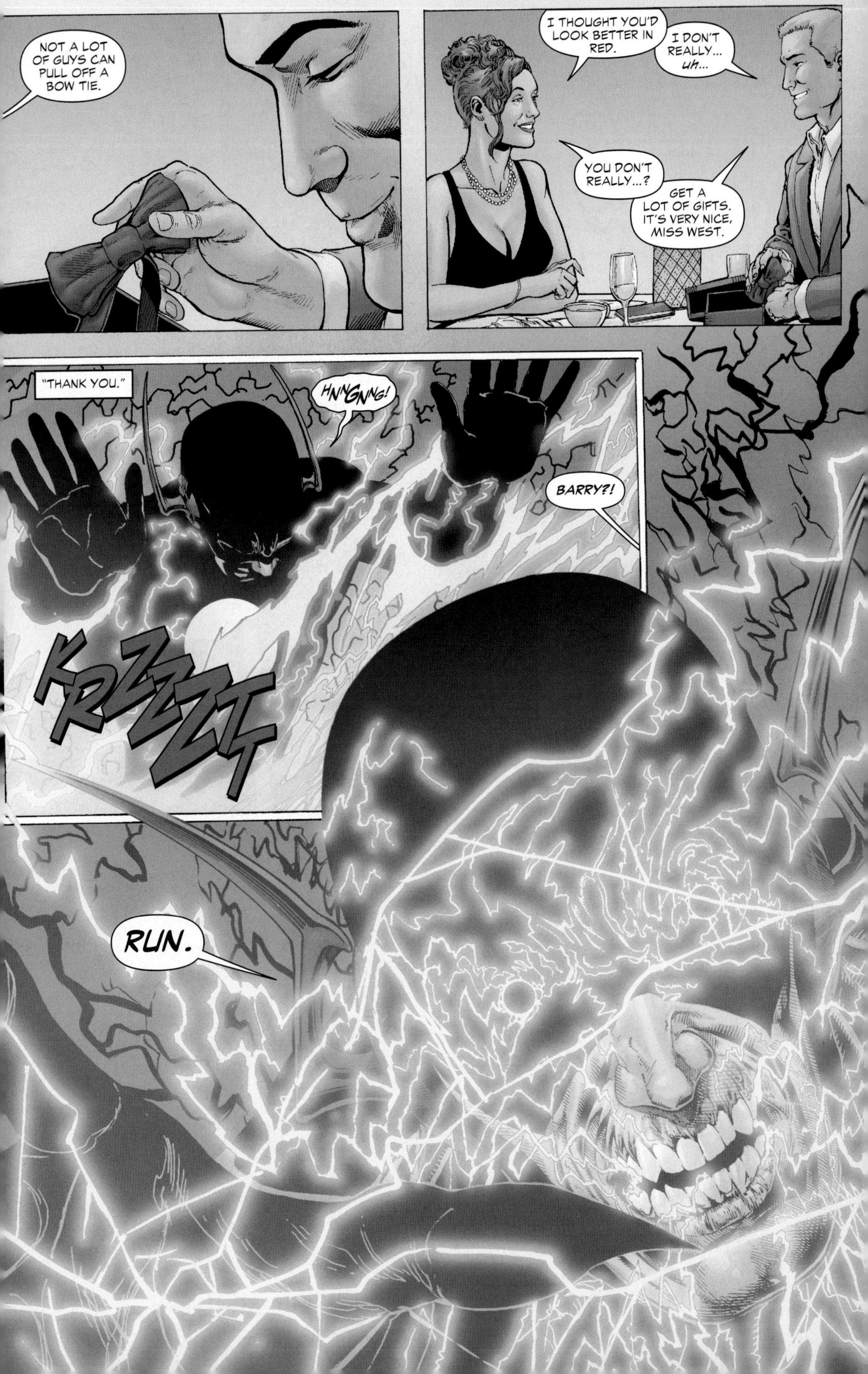

NOT A LOT OF GUYS CAN PULL OFF A BOW TIE.
I THOUGHT YOU'D LOOK BETTER IN RED.
I DON'T REALLY... *uh*...
YOU DON'T REALLY...?
GET A LOT OF GIFTS. IT'S VERY NICE, MISS WEST.
"THANK YOU."
HNNGNNG!
BARRY?!
KRZZZZT
RUN.

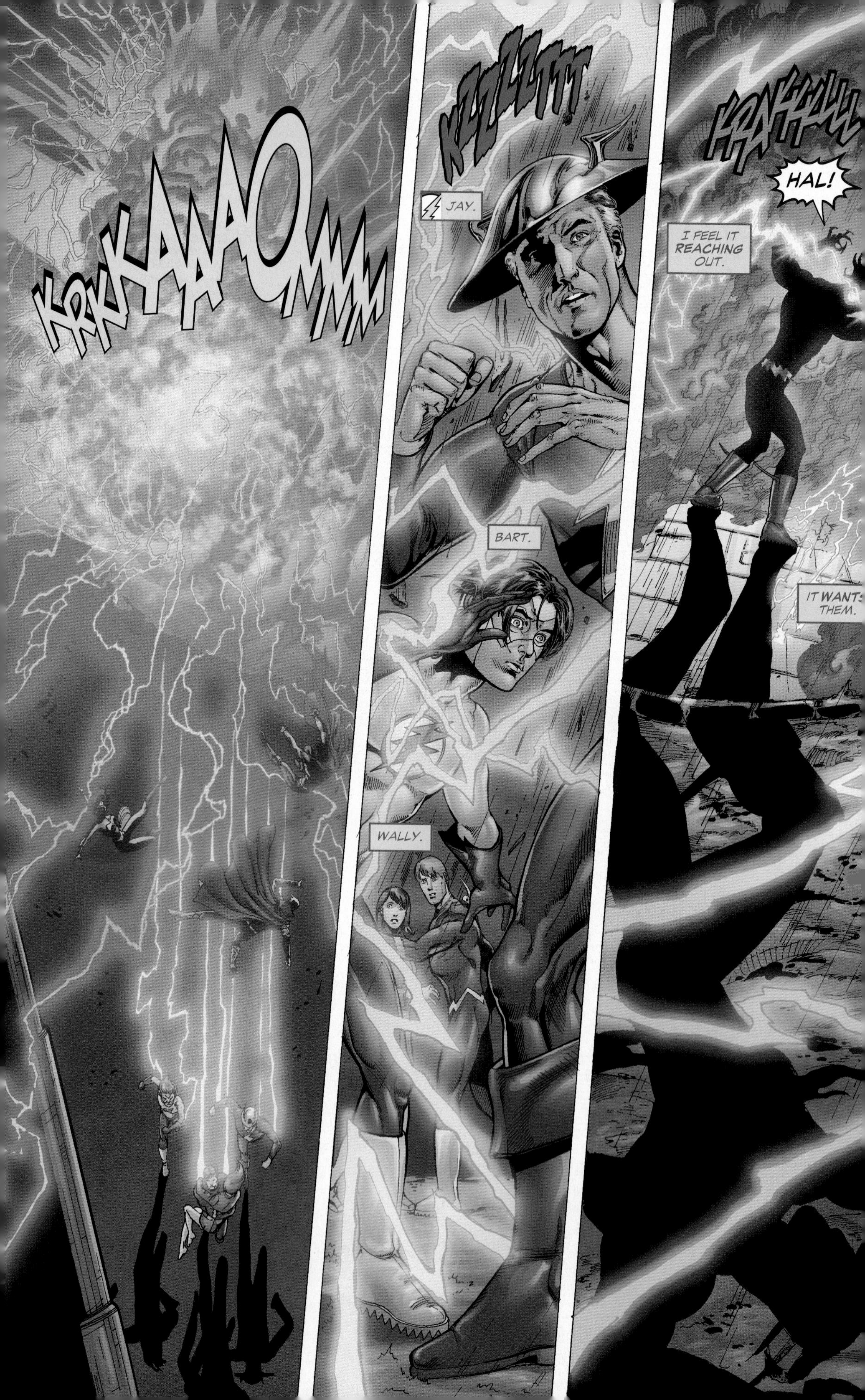
KRKKAAAOMMMM
KZZZZZTTT
JAY.
BART.
WALLY.
KRAKHUUU
HAL!
I FEEL IT REACHING OUT.
IT WANTS THEM.

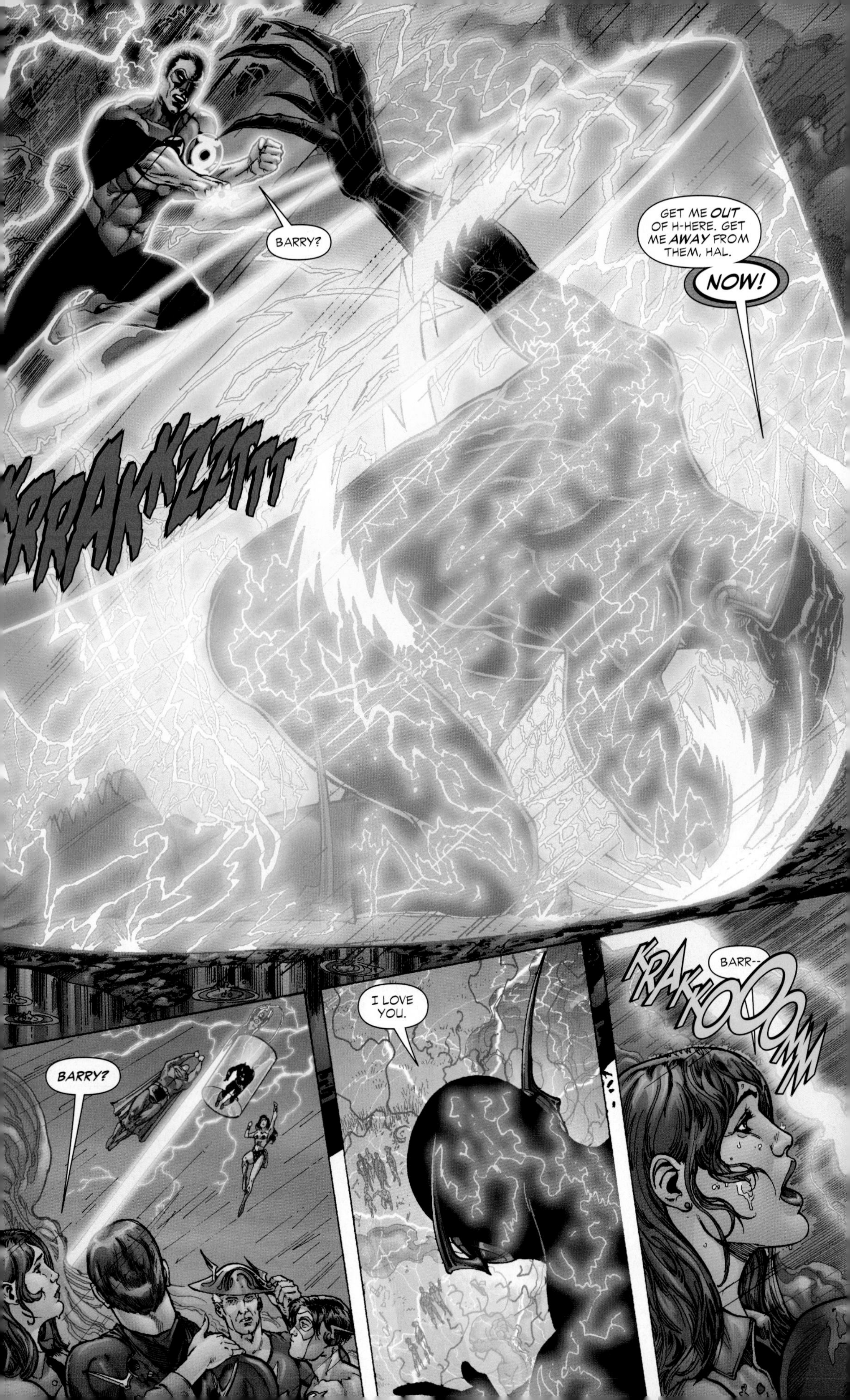
BARRY?
GET ME OUT OF H-HERE. GET ME AWAY FROM THEM, HAL.
NOW!
KRRAKKZZTTT
BARRY?
I LOVE YOU.
BARR--
KRAKOOOOMM

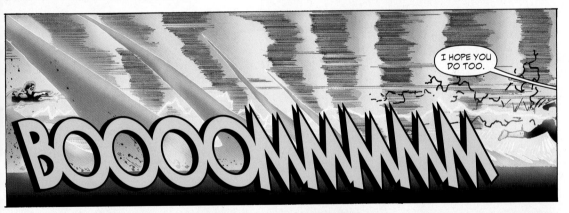

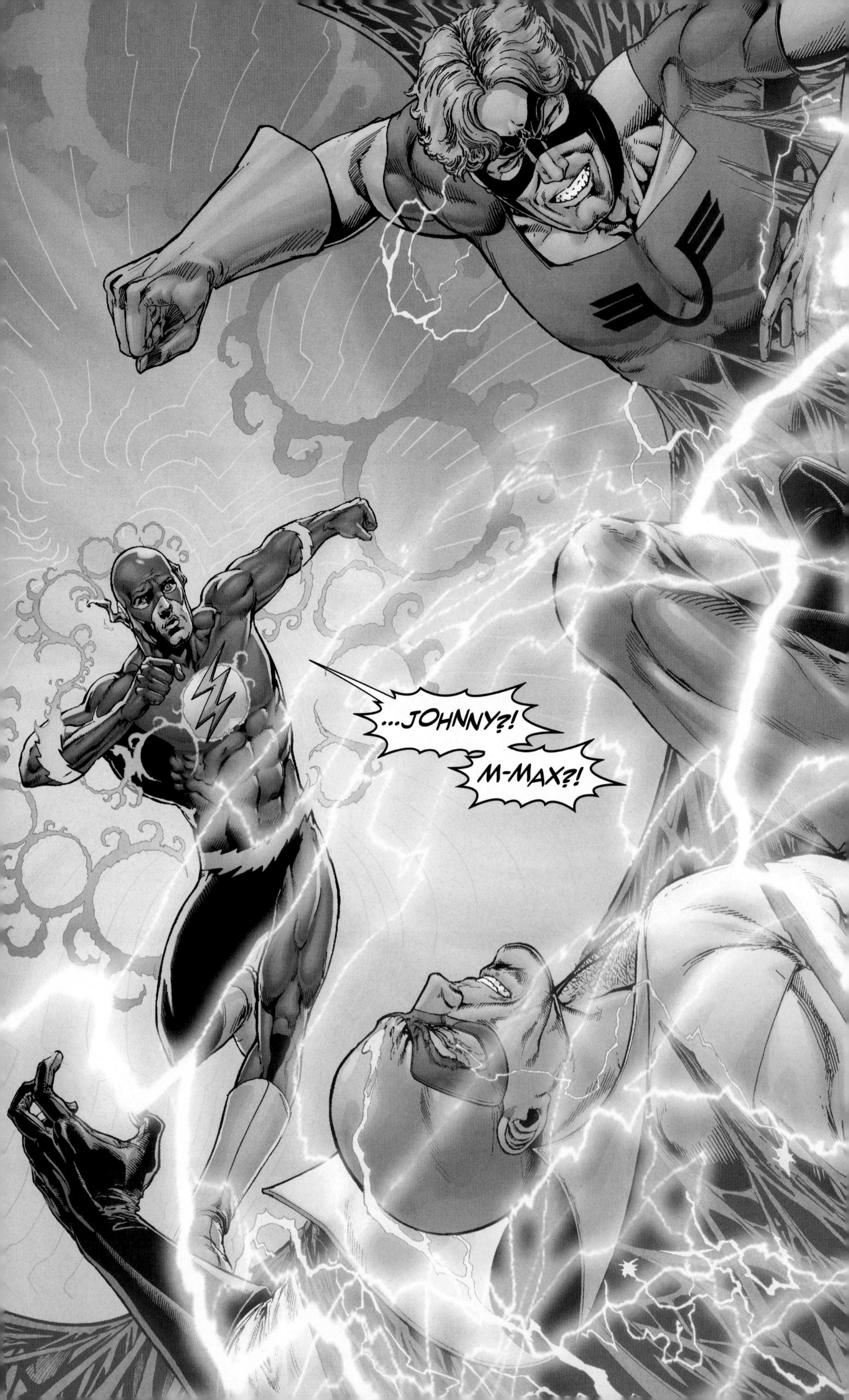
...JOHNNY?!
M-MAX?!

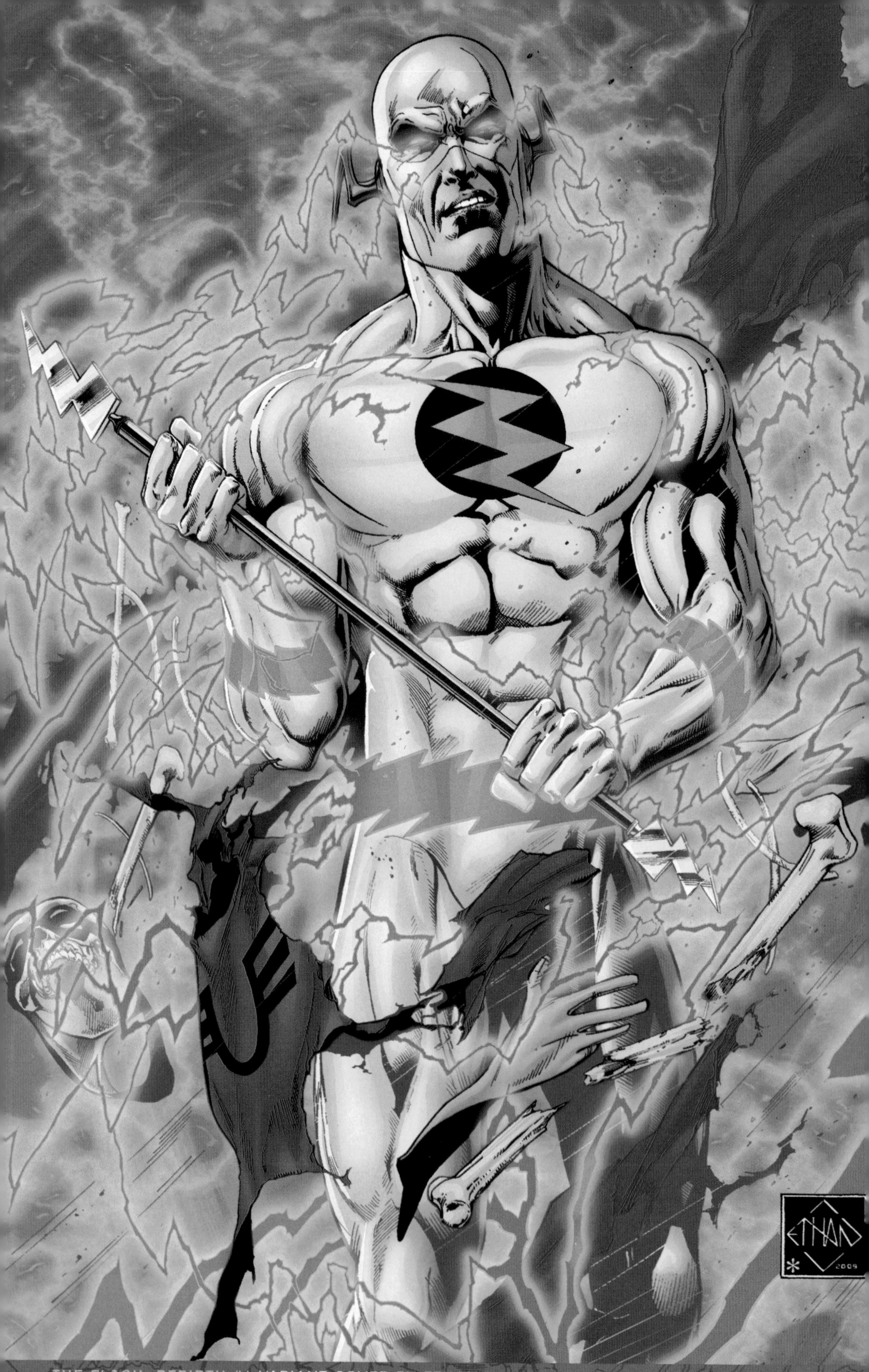
ETHAN

THE FLASH: REBIRTH #4 VARIANT COVER BY **ETHAN VAN SCIVER** WITH **BRIAN MILLER** OF **HI-FI**

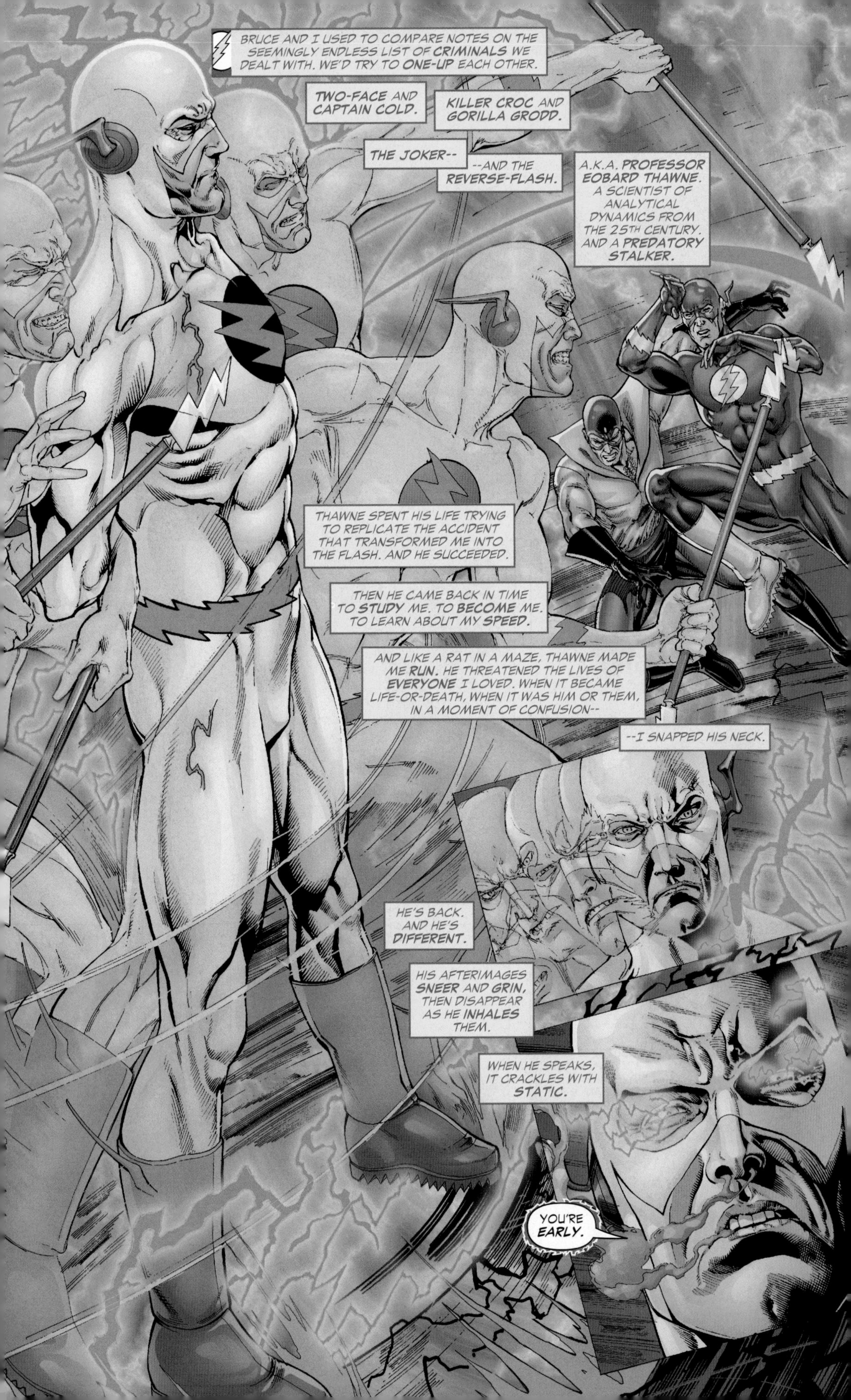
BRUCE AND I USED TO COMPARE NOTES ON THE SEEMINGLY ENDLESS LIST OF CRIMINALS WE DEALT WITH. WE'D TRY TO ONE-UP EACH OTHER.
TWO-FACE AND CAPTAIN COLD.
KILLER CROC AND GORILLA GRODD.
THE JOKER--
--AND THE REVERSE-FLASH.
A.K.A. PROFESSOR EOBARD THAWNE. A SCIENTIST OF ANALYTICAL DYNAMICS FROM THE 25TH CENTURY. AND A PREDATORY STALKER.
THAWNE SPENT HIS LIFE TRYING TO REPLICATE THE ACCIDENT THAT TRANSFORMED ME INTO THE FLASH. AND HE SUCCEEDED.
THEN HE CAME BACK IN TIME TO STUDY ME. TO BECOME ME. TO LEARN ABOUT MY SPEED.
AND LIKE A RAT IN A MAZE, THAWNE MADE ME RUN. HE THREATENED THE LIVES OF EVERYONE I LOVED. WHEN IT BECAME LIFE-OR-DEATH, WHEN IT WAS HIM OR THEM, IN A MOMENT OF CONFUSION--
--I SNAPPED HIS NECK.
HE'S BACK. AND HE'S DIFFERENT.
HIS AFTERIMAGES SNEER AND GRIN, THEN DISAPPEAR AS HE INHALES THEM.
WHEN HE SPEAKS, IT CRACKLES WITH STATIC.
YOU'RE EARLY.

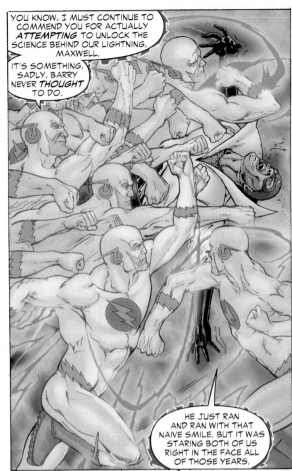

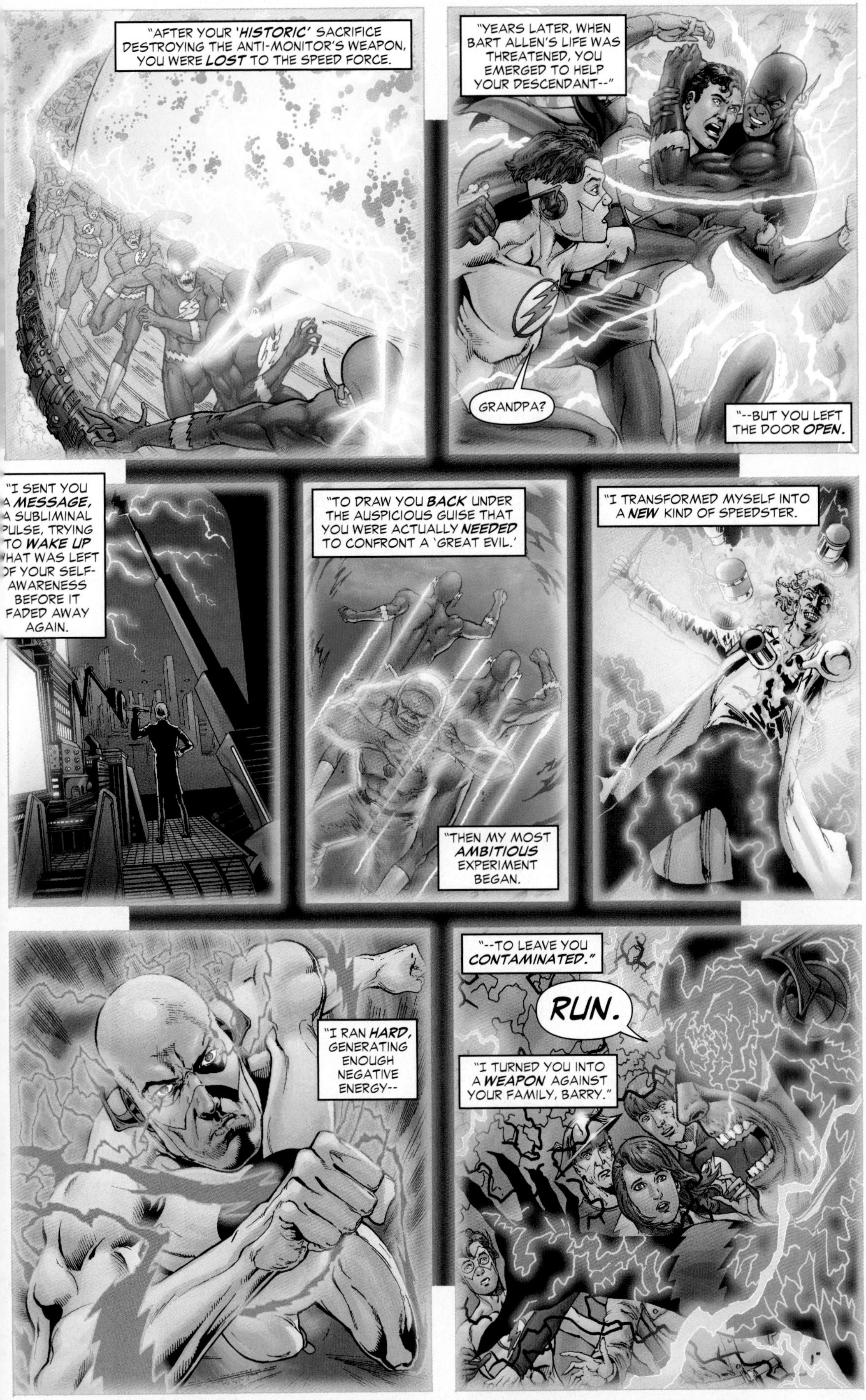
"AFTER YOUR 'HISTORIC' SACRIFICE DESTROYING THE ANTI-MONITOR'S WEAPON, YOU WERE LOST TO THE SPEED FORCE.
"YEARS LATER, WHEN BART ALLEN'S LIFE WAS THREATENED, YOU EMERGED TO HELP YOUR DESCENDANT--"
GRANDPA?
"--BUT YOU LEFT THE DOOR OPEN.
"I SENT YOU A MESSAGE, A SUBLIMINAL PULSE, TRYING TO WAKE UP WHAT WAS LEFT OF YOUR SELF-AWARENESS BEFORE IT FADED AWAY AGAIN.
"TO DRAW YOU BACK UNDER THE AUSPICIOUS GUISE THAT YOU WERE ACTUALLY NEEDED TO CONFRONT A 'GREAT EVIL.'
"THEN MY MOST AMBITIOUS EXPERIMENT BEGAN.
"I TRANSFORMED MYSELF INTO A NEW KIND OF SPEEDSTER.
"I RAN HARD, GENERATING ENOUGH NEGATIVE ENERGY--
"--TO LEAVE YOU CONTAMINATED."
RUN.
"I TURNED YOU INTO A WEAPON AGAINST YOUR FAMILY, BARRY."

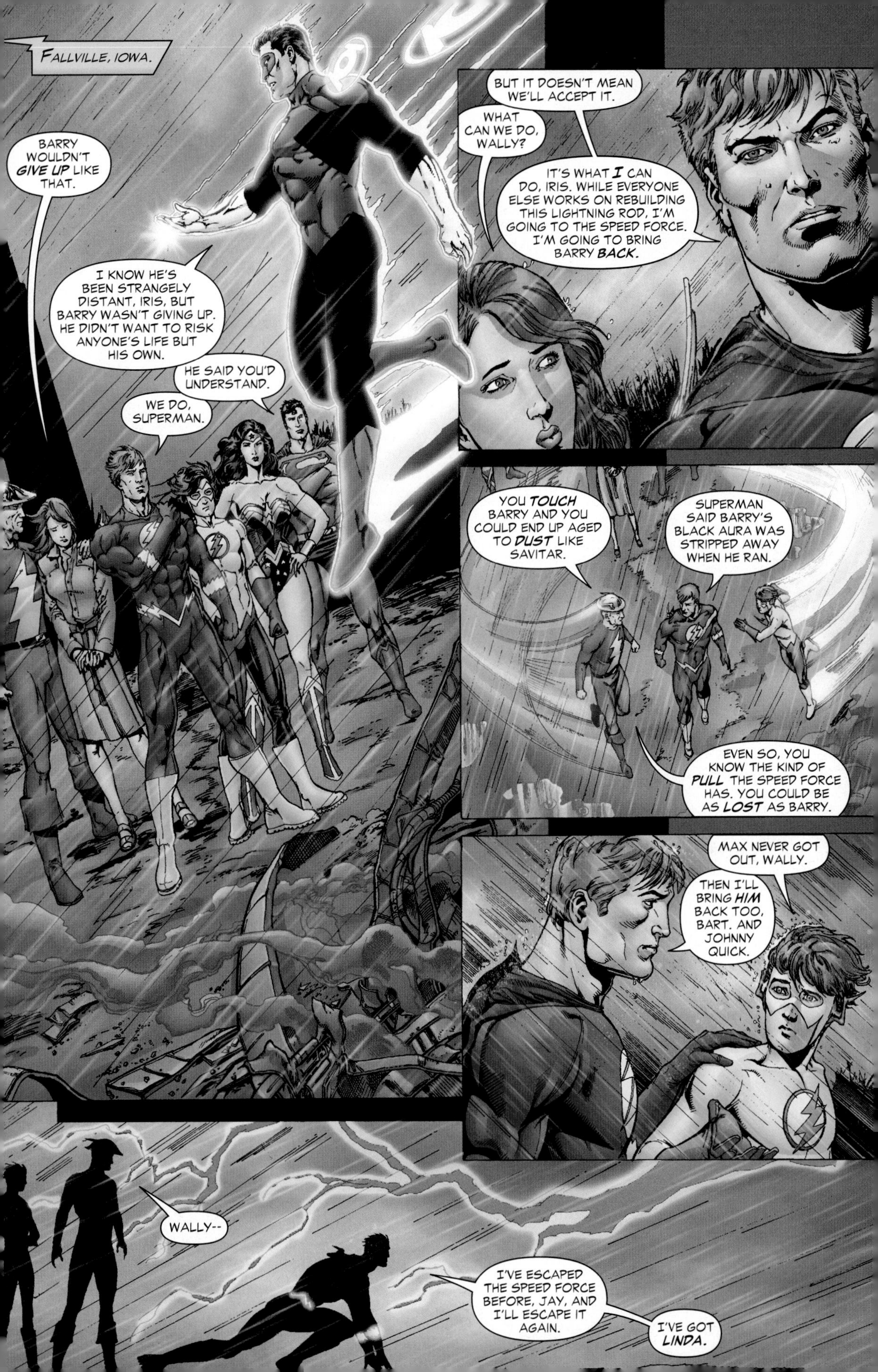
FALLVILLE, IOWA.
BARRY WOULDN'T GIVE UP LIKE THAT.
I KNOW HE'S BEEN STRANGELY DISTANT, IRIS, BUT BARRY WASN'T GIVING UP. HE DIDN'T WANT TO RISK ANYONE'S LIFE BUT HIS OWN.
HE SAID YOU'D UNDERSTAND.
WE DO, SUPERMAN.
BUT IT DOESN'T MEAN WE'LL ACCEPT IT.
WHAT CAN WE DO, WALLY?
IT'S WHAT I CAN DO, IRIS. WHILE EVERYONE ELSE WORKS ON REBUILDING THIS LIGHTNING ROD, I'M GOING TO THE SPEED FORCE. I'M GOING TO BRING BARRY BACK.
YOU TOUCH BARRY AND YOU COULD END UP AGED TO DUST LIKE SAVITAR.
SUPERMAN SAID BARRY'S BLACK AURA WAS STRIPPED AWAY WHEN HE RAN.
EVEN SO, YOU KNOW THE KIND OF PULL THE SPEED FORCE HAS. YOU COULD BE AS LOST AS BARRY.
MAX NEVER GOT OUT, WALLY.
THEN I'LL BRING HIM BACK TOO, BART. AND JOHNNY QUICK.
WALLY--
I'VE ESCAPED THE SPEED FORCE BEFORE, JAY, AND I'LL ESCAPE IT AGAIN.
I'VE GOT LINDA.

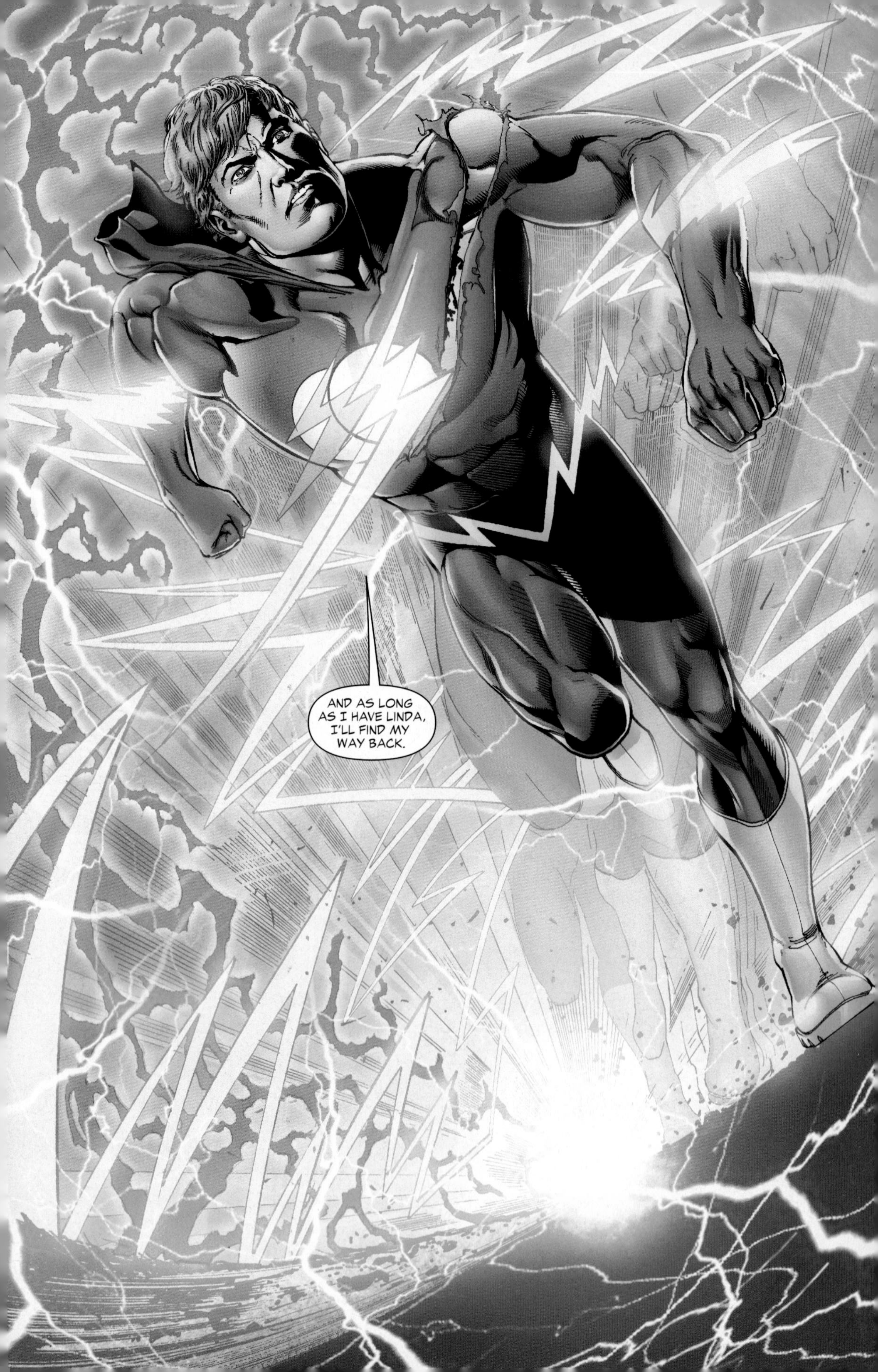
AND AS LONG AS I HAVE LINDA, I'LL FIND MY WAY BACK.

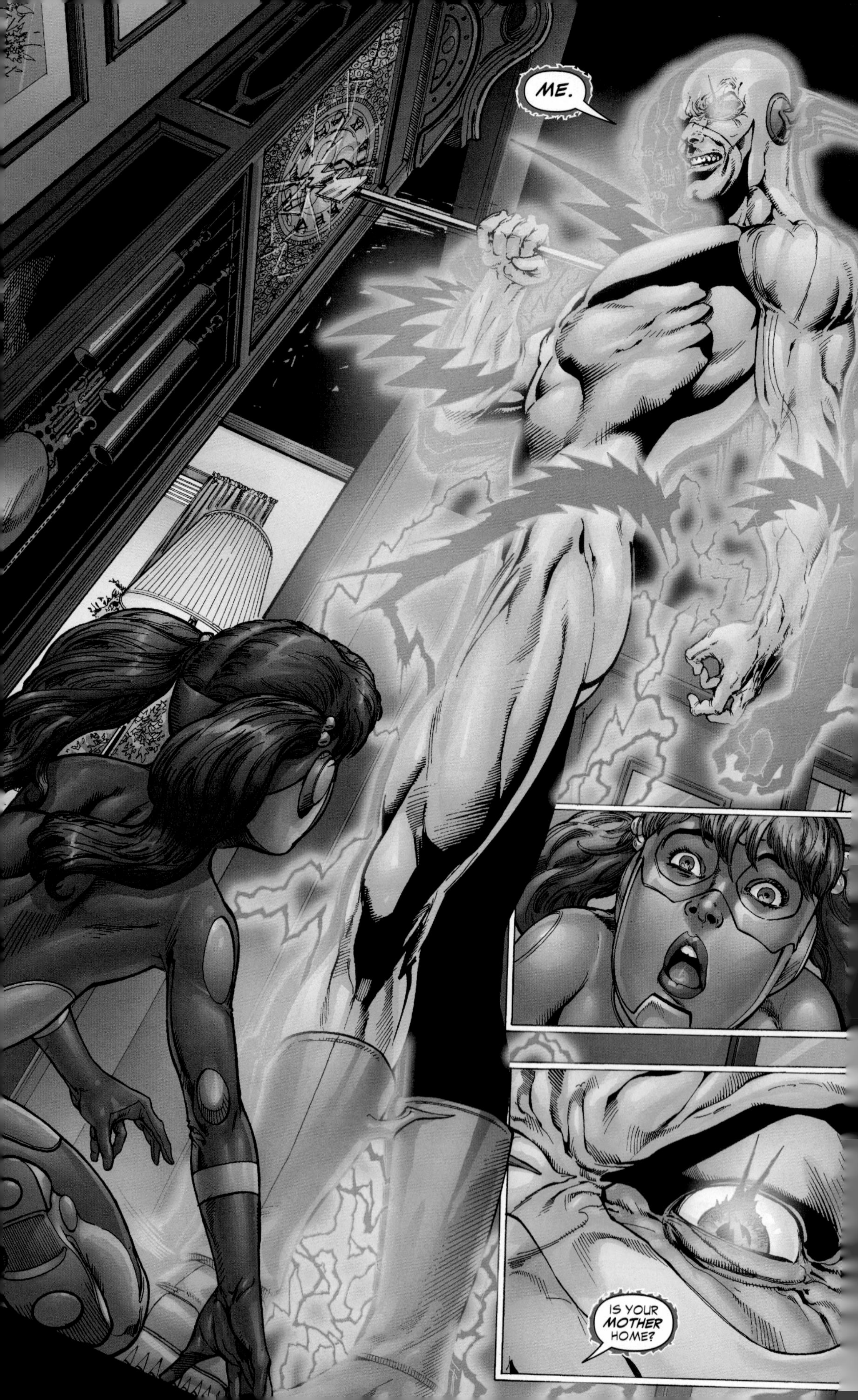
ME.
IS YOUR MOTHER HOME?

THE SPEED FORCE.

CONGRATULATIONS, MR. AND MRS. WEST.

IT'S A **BOY** AND A **GIRL**. YOU'VE JUST HAD **TWINS**.

BART! BART-- **WAIT!**

THAWNE'S LIGHTNING IS CORRUPTING ME. WE NEED TO FIND A WAY **OUT** OF HERE, MAX.

I CAN'T GET OUT, BARRY.

WHAT?

JAY HAS **JOAN**. WALLY HAS **LINDA**. YOU HAVE **IRIS**.

ALL THE SPEEDSTERS, WHEN THEY'RE PUSHED TO THE **LIMITS**--

"--THEY **NEED** A LIGHTNING ROD TO GROUND THEM."

THE HEADQUARTERS OF THE JUSTICE SOCIETY OF AMERICA.

$3 \times 2(9YZ)4A = ?$

$3 \times 2(9YZ)4A = ?$

$3 \times 2(9YZ)4A = ?$

WHAT HAPPENED?

AS SOON AS HER FATHER FADED AWAY, SHE STARTED SAYING HIS **SPEED FORMULA** OVER AND OVER.

HELP'S COMING. JUST HOLD ON, JESS. HOLD ON FOR ME, BABE.

I NEVER HAD AN **ANCHOR**. AND JOHNNY **LOST** LIBBY. THAT'S WHY NEITHER OF US C-COULD **ESCAPE**. BUT YOU...

I CAN'T **RUN** OUT OF HERE, MAX. I'M **CUT OFF** FROM THE SPEED FORCE.

NO, YOU'RE **NOT**. YOU'RE **NOT** LIKE THE REST OF US, BARRY.

YOU'RE LIKE **THAWNE**.

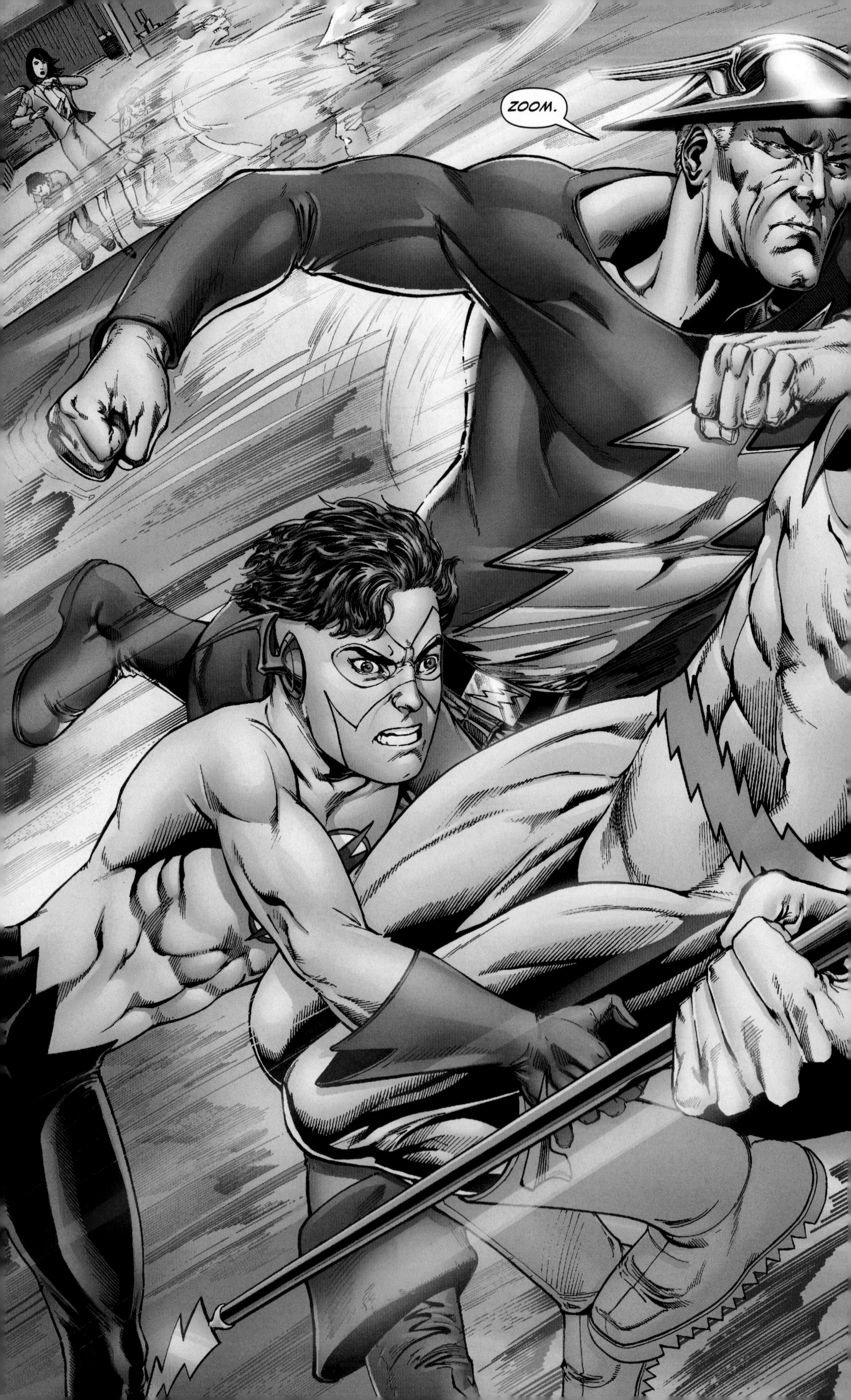
ZOOM.

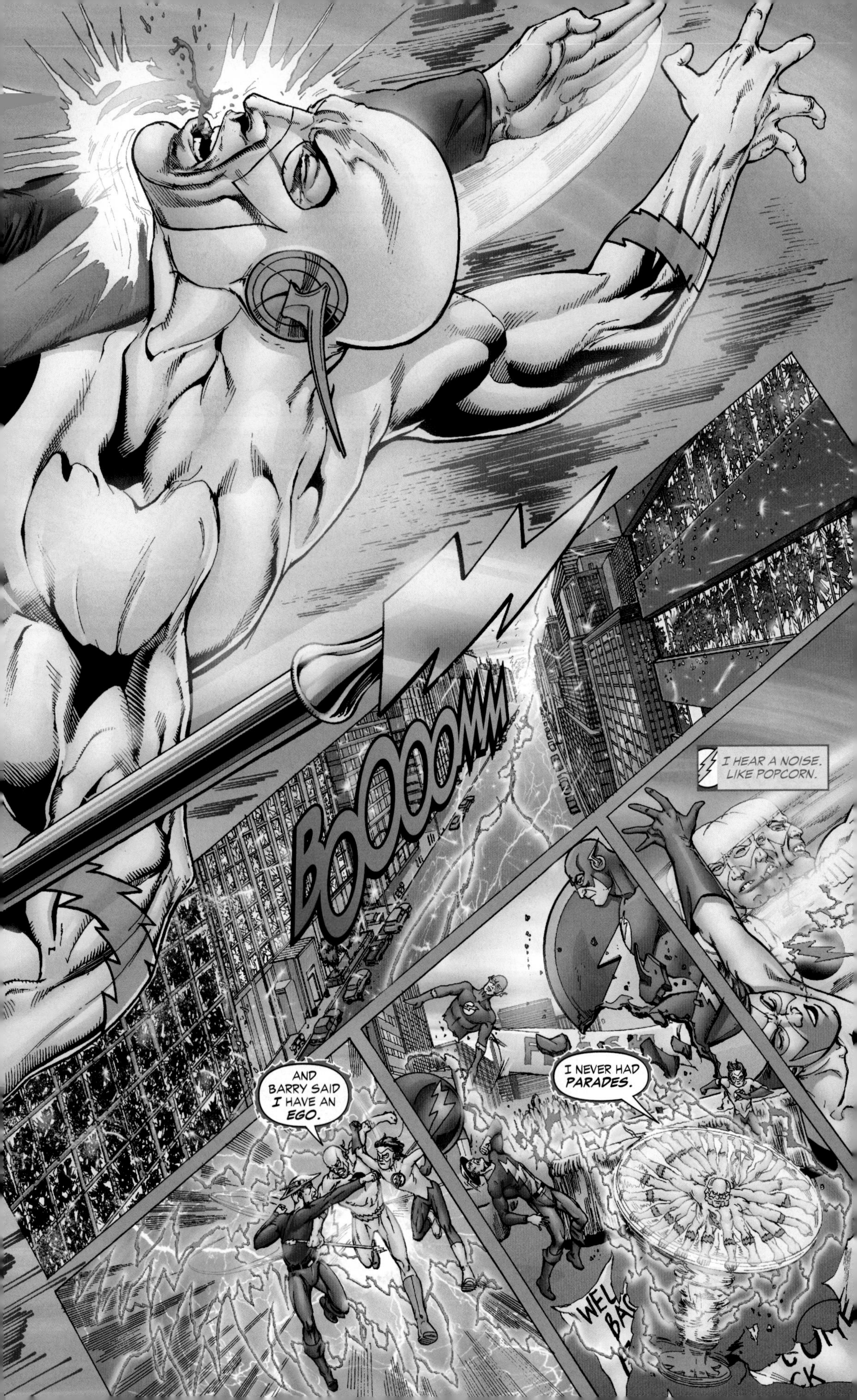
BOOOOMM
I HEAR A NOISE. LIKE POPCORN.
AND BARRY SAID I HAVE AN EGO.
I NEVER HAD PARADES.

THE FLASH: REBIRTH #5 COVER BY ETHAN VAN SCIVER
(AFTER CARMINE INFANTINO) WITH BRIAN MILLER OF HI-FI

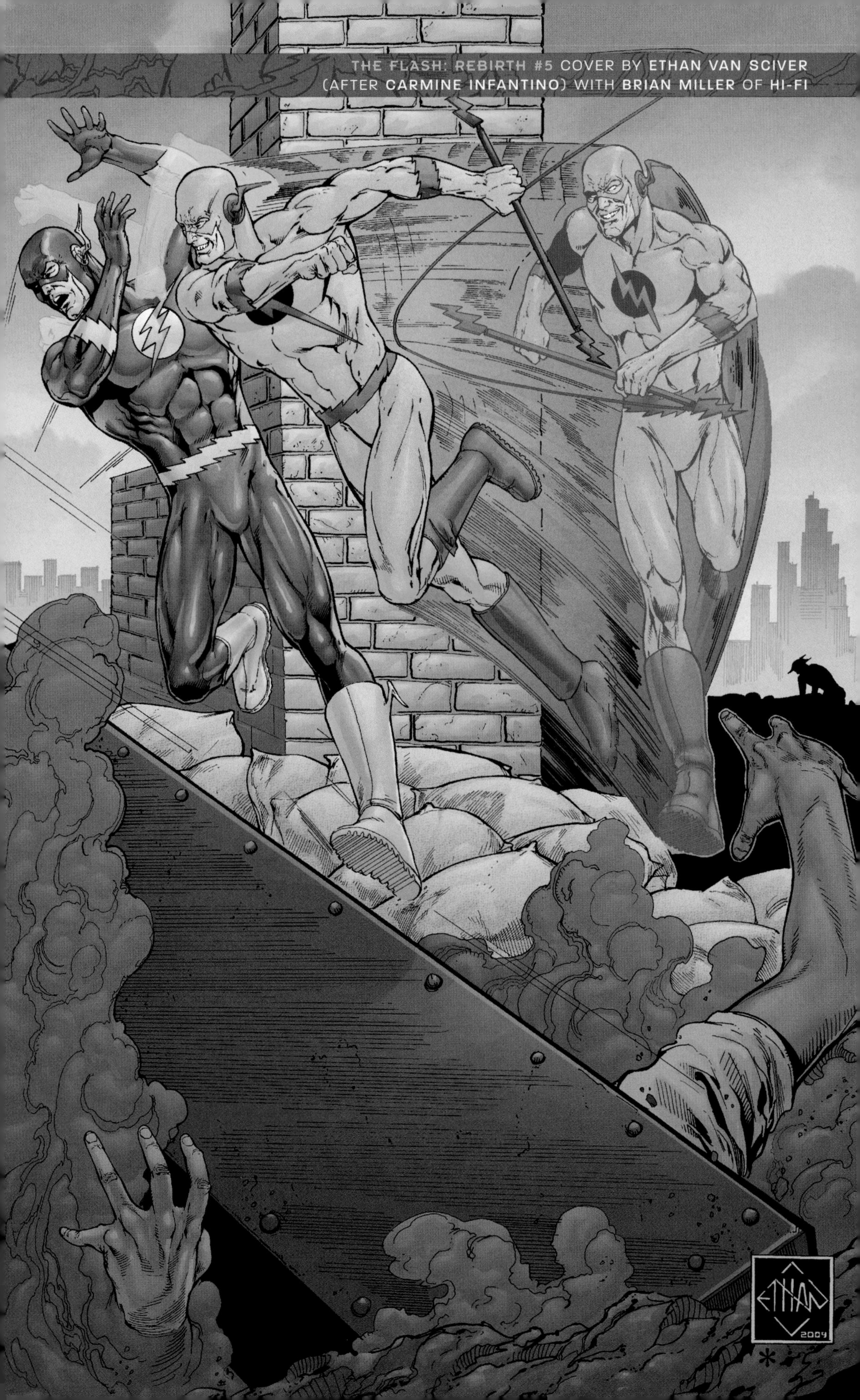
ETHAN
2009

THE FLASH: REBIRTH #5 VARIANT COVER BY **ETHAN VAN SCIVER** WITH **BRIAN MILLER** OF **HI-FI**

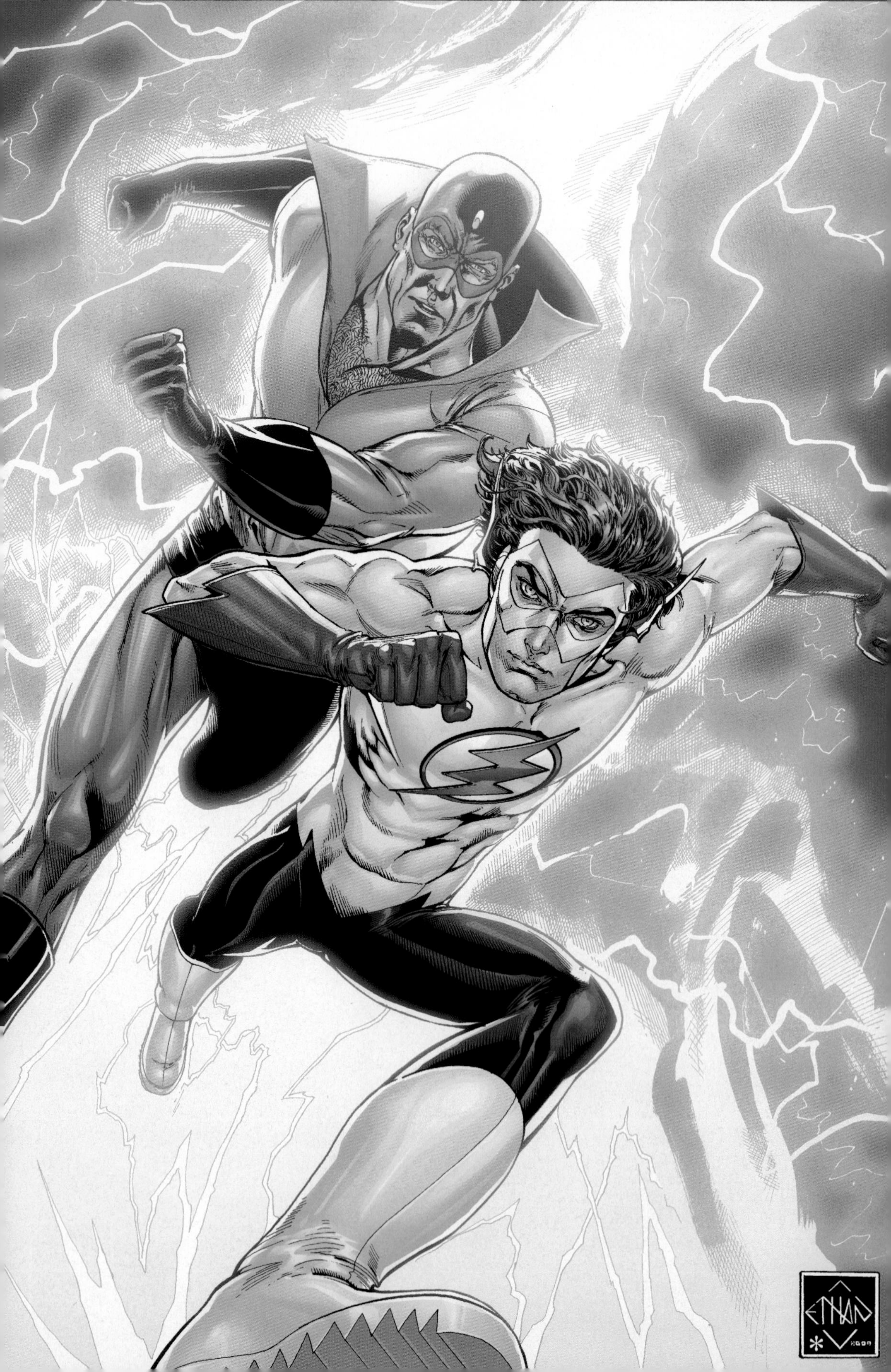

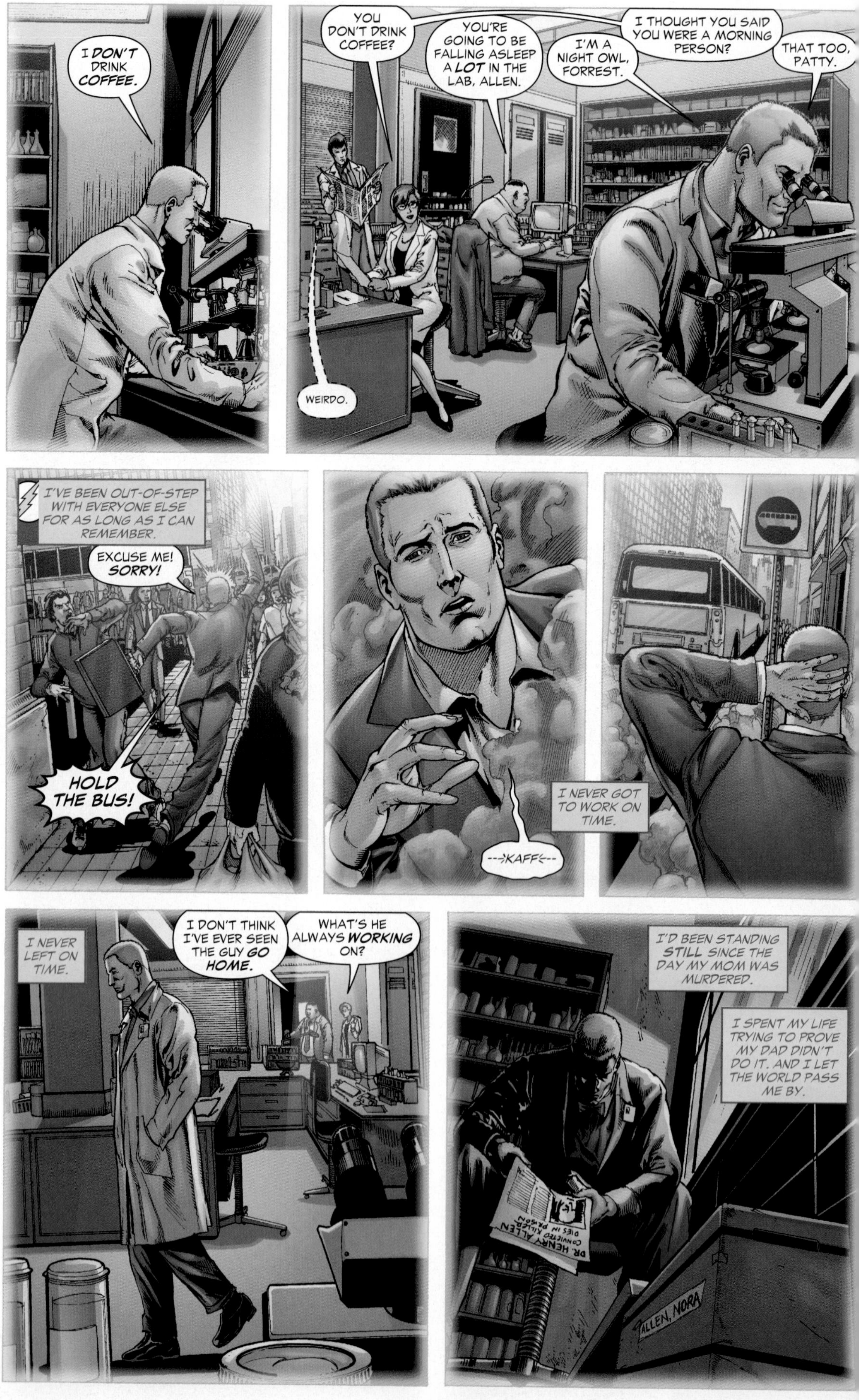
I DON'T DRINK COFFEE.
YOU DON'T DRINK COFFEE?
YOU'RE GOING TO BE FALLING ASLEEP A LOT IN THE LAB, ALLEN.
I'M A NIGHT OWL, FORREST.
I THOUGHT YOU SAID YOU WERE A MORNING PERSON?
THAT TOO, PATTY.
WEIRDO.
I'VE BEEN OUT-OF-STEP WITH EVERYONE ELSE FOR AS LONG AS I CAN REMEMBER.
EXCUSE ME! SORRY!
HOLD THE BUS!
KAFF
I NEVER GOT TO WORK ON TIME.
I NEVER LEFT ON TIME.
I DON'T THINK I'VE EVER SEEN THE GUY GO HOME.
WHAT'S HE ALWAYS WORKING ON?
I'D BEEN STANDING STILL SINCE THE DAY MY MOM WAS MURDERED.
I SPENT MY LIFE TRYING TO PROVE MY DAD DIDN'T DO IT. AND I LET THE WORLD PASS ME BY.
DR. HENRY ALLEN CONVICTED KILLER DIES IN PRISON
ALLEN, NORA

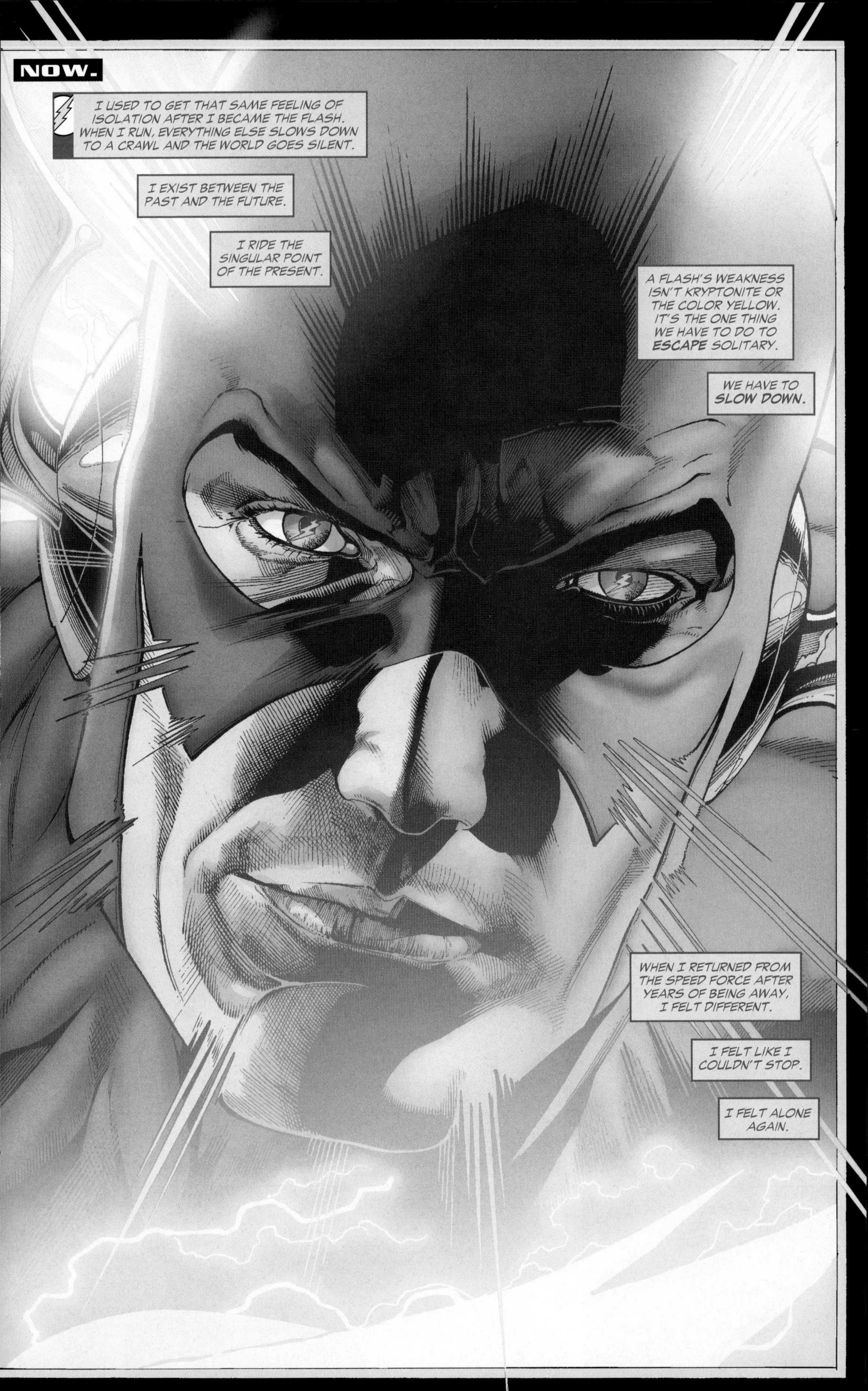
NOW.
I USED TO GET THAT SAME FEELING OF ISOLATION AFTER I BECAME THE FLASH. WHEN I RUN, EVERYTHING ELSE SLOWS DOWN TO A CRAWL AND THE WORLD GOES SILENT.
I EXIST BETWEEN THE PAST AND THE FUTURE.
I RIDE THE SINGULAR POINT OF THE PRESENT.
A FLASH'S WEAKNESS ISN'T KRYPTONITE OR THE COLOR YELLOW. IT'S THE ONE THING WE HAVE TO DO TO ESCAPE SOLITARY.
WE HAVE TO SLOW DOWN.
WHEN I RETURNED FROM THE SPEED FORCE AFTER YEARS OF BEING AWAY, I FELT DIFFERENT.
I FELT LIKE I COULDN'T STOP.
I FELT ALONE AGAIN.

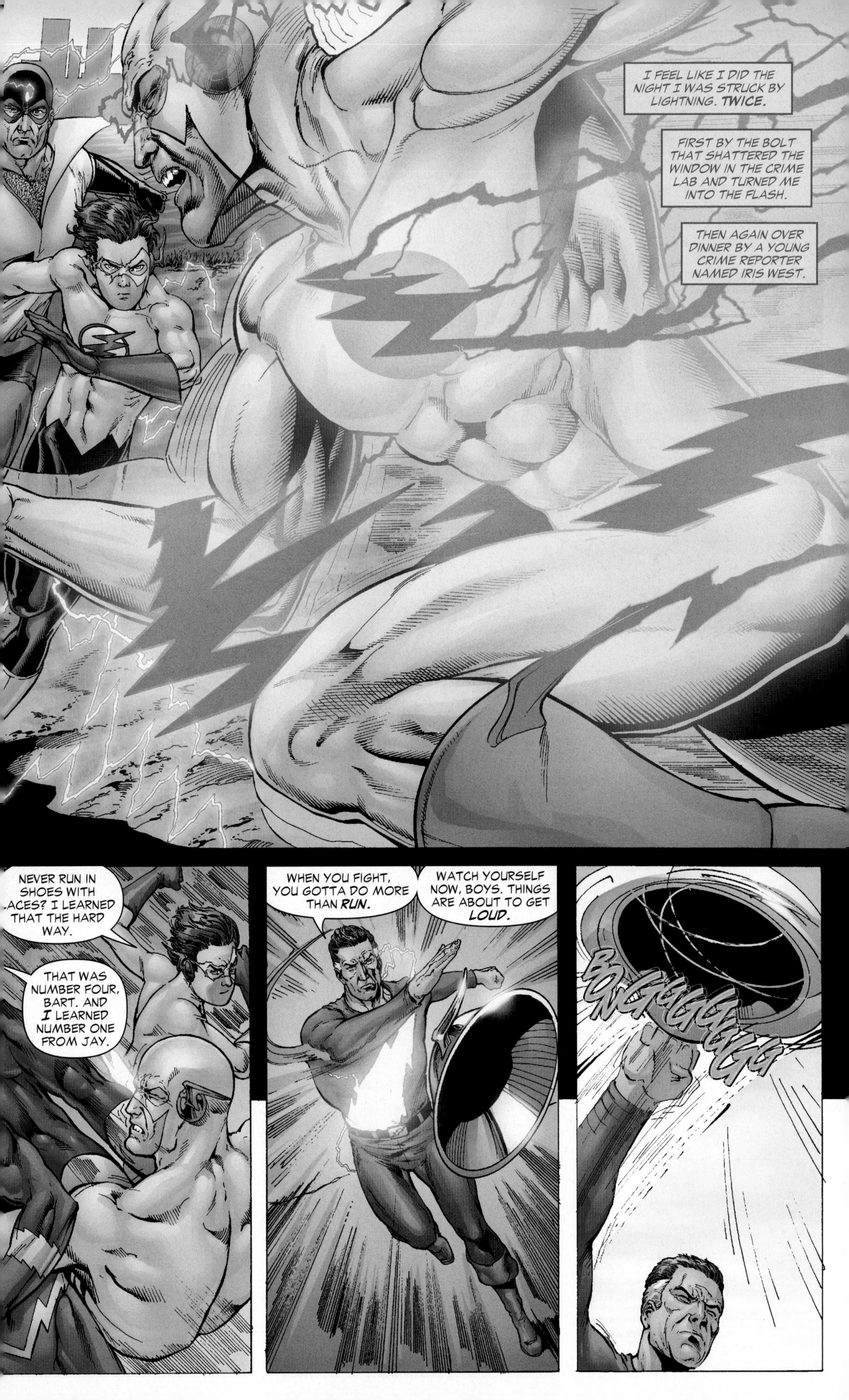
I FEEL LIKE I DID THE NIGHT I WAS STRUCK BY LIGHTNING. TWICE.
FIRST BY THE BOLT THAT SHATTERED THE WINDOW IN THE CRIME LAB AND TURNED ME INTO THE FLASH.
THEN AGAIN OVER DINNER BY A YOUNG CRIME REPORTER NAMED IRIS WEST.
NEVER RUN IN SHOES WITH LACES? I LEARNED THAT THE HARD WAY.
THAT WAS NUMBER FOUR, BART. AND I LEARNED NUMBER ONE FROM JAY.
WHEN YOU FIGHT, YOU GOTTA DO MORE THAN RUN.
WATCH YOURSELF NOW, BOYS. THINGS ARE ABOUT TO GET LOUD.
BONGGGGGG

JAY SETS OFF A SONIC BOMB.

WE OUTRUN THE SOUND WAVES.

AND AS LONG AS THAWNE'S FEET DON'T TOUCH THE GROUND--

--HE DOESN'T HAVE ANY TRACTION TO FOLLOW US.

Welcome to CENTRAL CITY

THE FASTEST CITY IN THE WEST

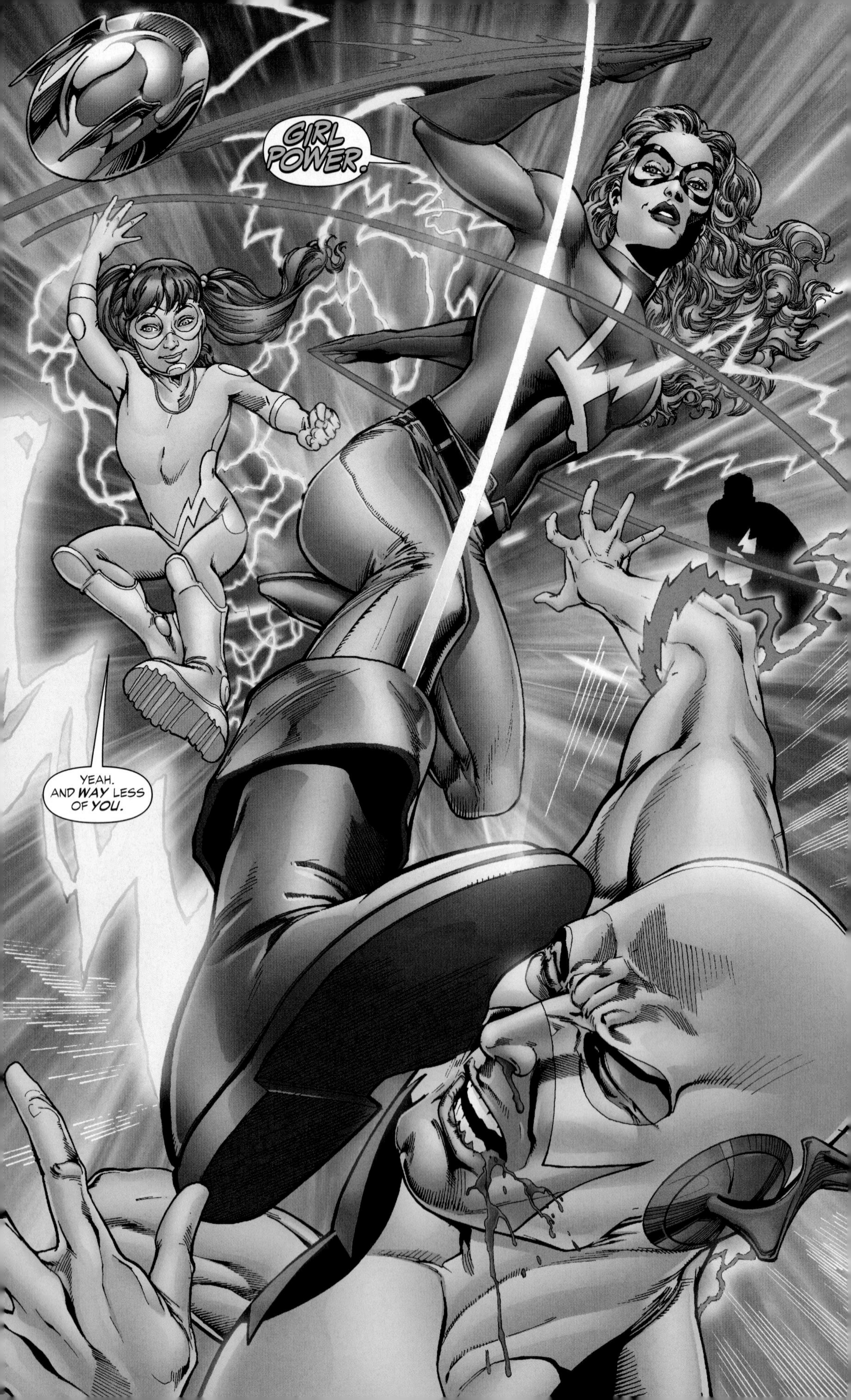
GIRL POWER.
YEAH. AND WAY LESS OF YOU.

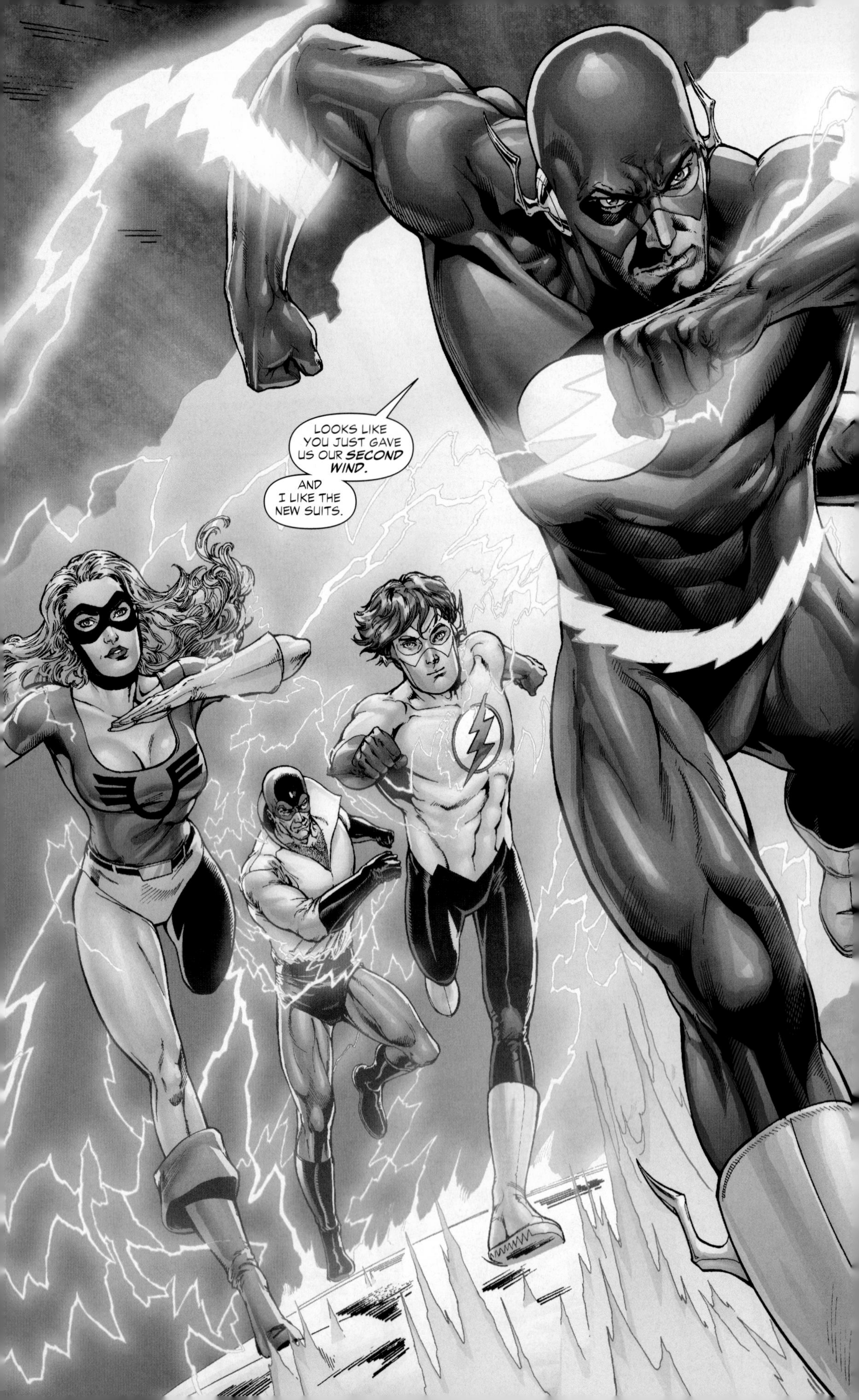
LOOKS LIKE YOU JUST GAVE US OUR SECOND WIND.
AND I LIKE THE NEW SUITS.

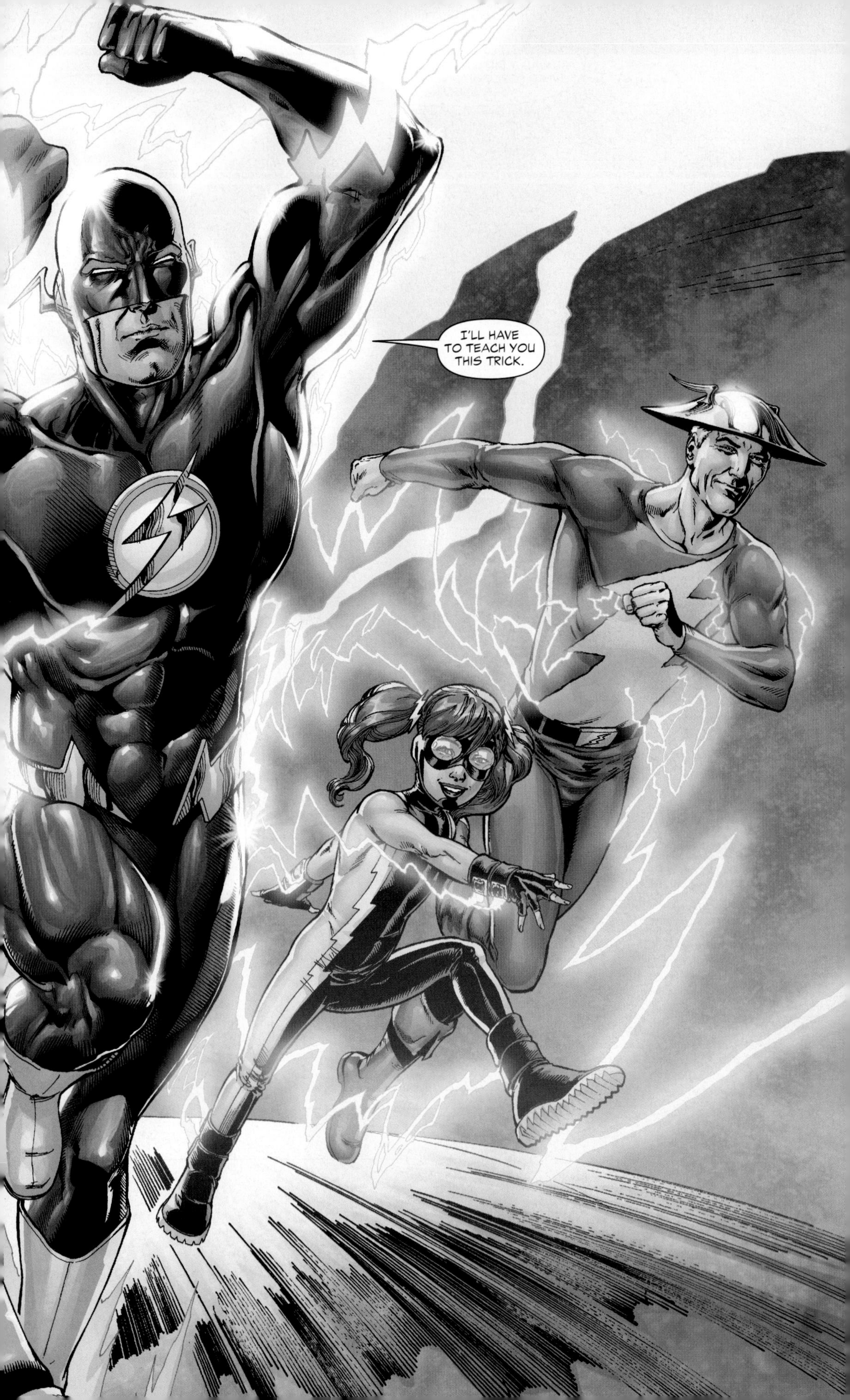
I'LL HAVE TO TEACH YOU THIS TRICK.

BRRRRNNNGGGGG

OH, NO. I'M--

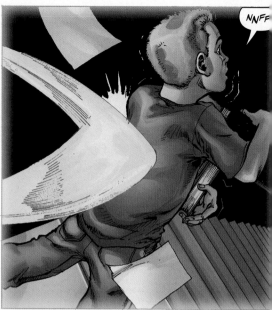

NNFF

AAHH!

KRAK AAK

"SOMEONE PUSHED YOU DOWN THE STAIRS IN SCHOOL.

"BUT WHEN YOU LOOKED BACK--

"--NO ONE WAS THERE."

DO YOU REMEMBER THE ELECTRICAL FIRE THAT BURNED DOWN YOUR FIRST HOUSE IN FALLVILLE? OR THE DAY YOU MOVED TO CENTRAL CITY AND YOU LEFT THE BACK DOOR OPEN? YOUR DOG RAN OUT AND GOT HIT BY A CAR.

WHAT IF EVERY *BAD THING* THAT HAPPENED TO YOU WAS *ORCHESTRATED* BY ONE PERSON?

BY AN ENEMY YOU HADN'T EVEN *MADE* YET?

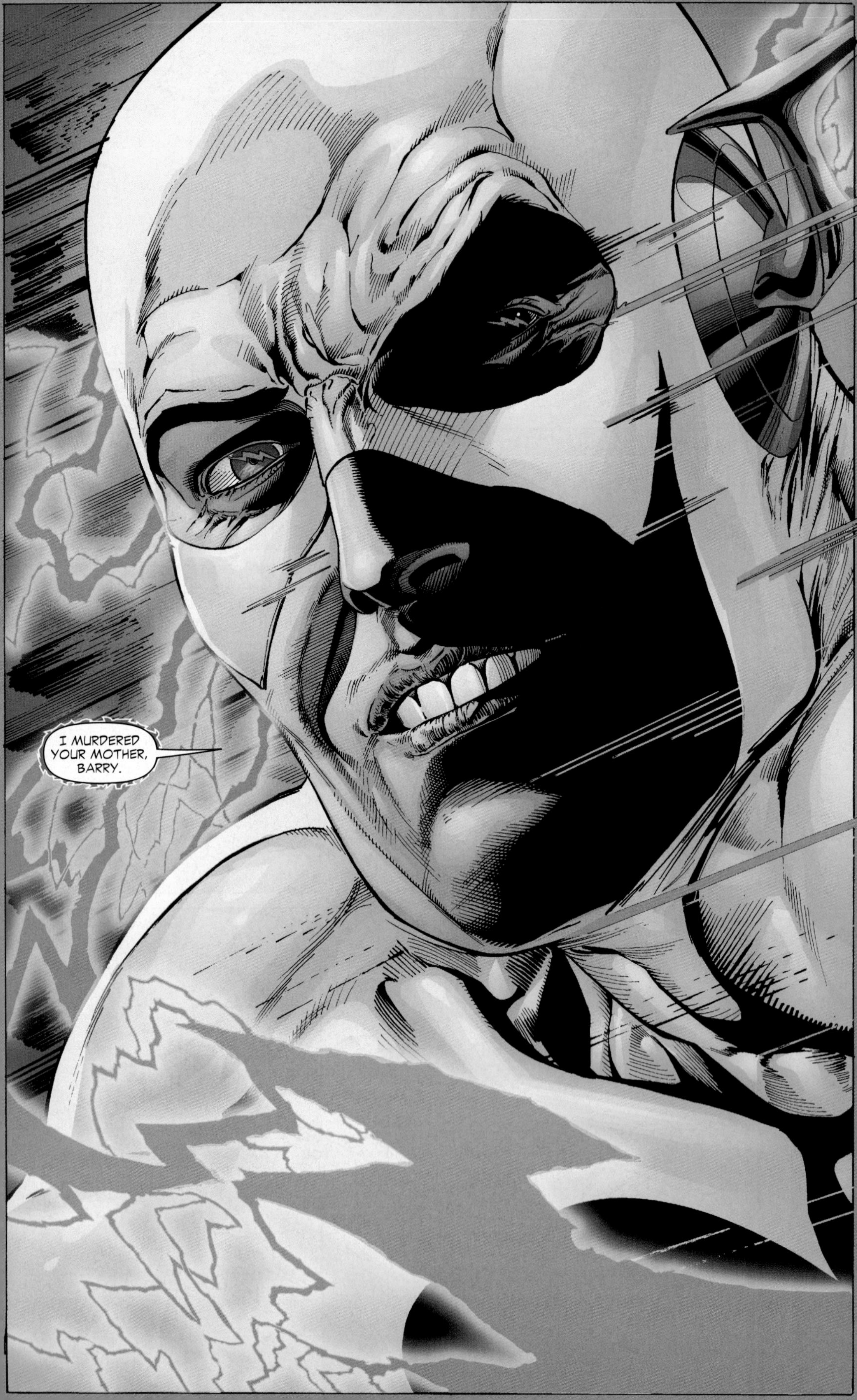
I MURDERED YOUR MOTHER, BARRY.

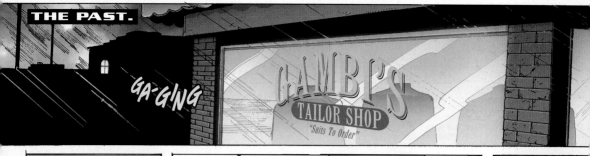

THE PAST.

GA-GING

GAMBI'S
TAILOR SHOP
"Suits To Order"

GOOD EVENING.

A LITTLE LATE FOR COFFEE, ISN'T IT?

IF I'M AWAKE, I'M DRINKING IT. IT'S BEEN A PROBLEM SINCE THE THIRD GRADE.

WHAT CAN I HELP YOU WITH, MISS?

IT'S ON SPECIAL.

I WANTED TO GET A GIFT FOR SOMEONE I'M MEETING TONIGHT. SORT OF AN APOLOGY FOR PUTTING MY FOOT IN MY MOUTH. WHICH I DO. A LOT.

ANYTHING SPECIFIC IN MIND?

DO YOU HAVE ANY BOW TIES?

I WAS THINKING SOMETHING IN RED.

AS LONG AS I KILL IRIS--

--EVERYTHING WILL BE ALL RIGHT.

MOTHER, MAY I

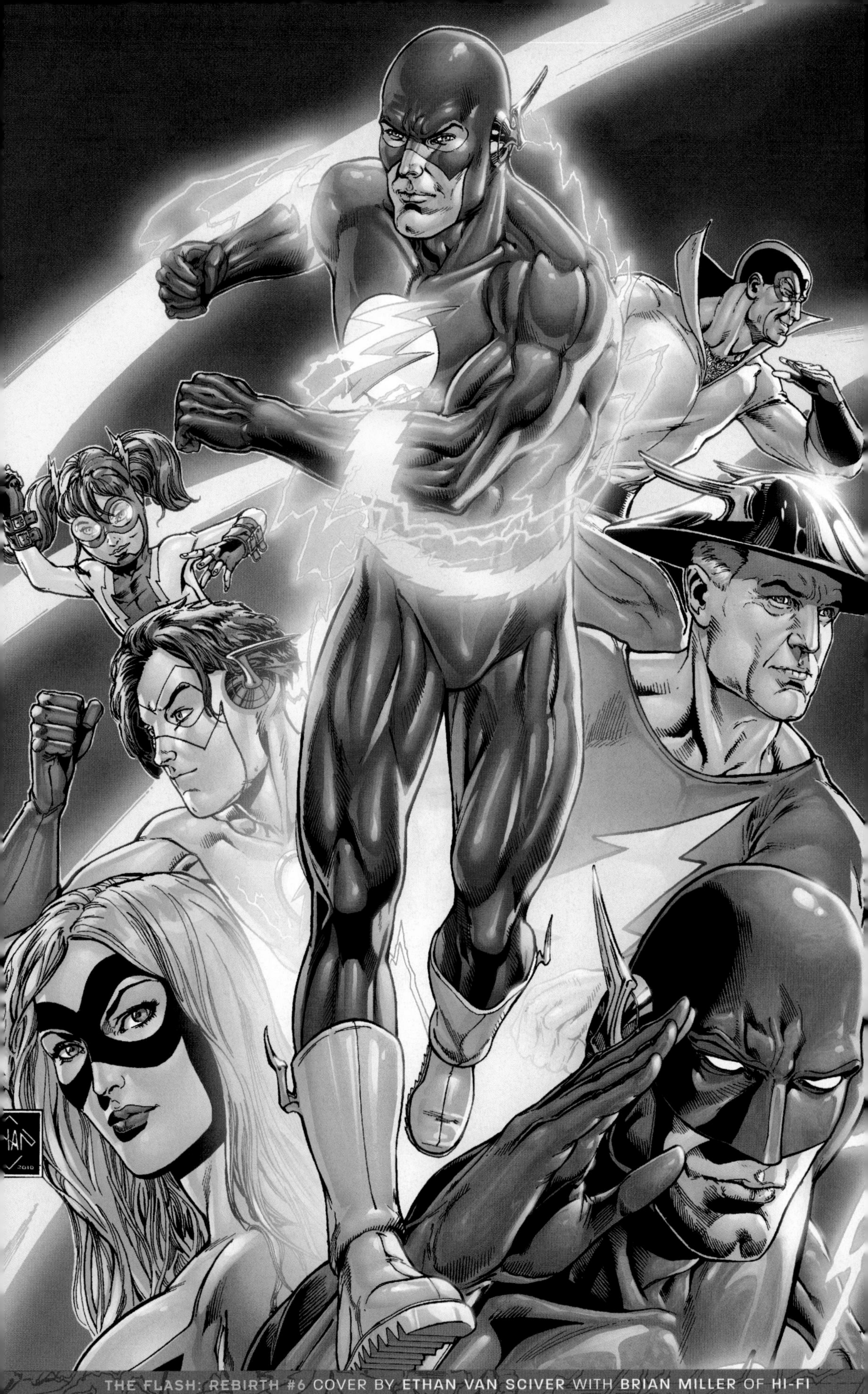

THE FLASH: REBIRTH #6 COVER BY ETHAN VAN SCIVER WITH BRIAN MILLER OF HI-FI

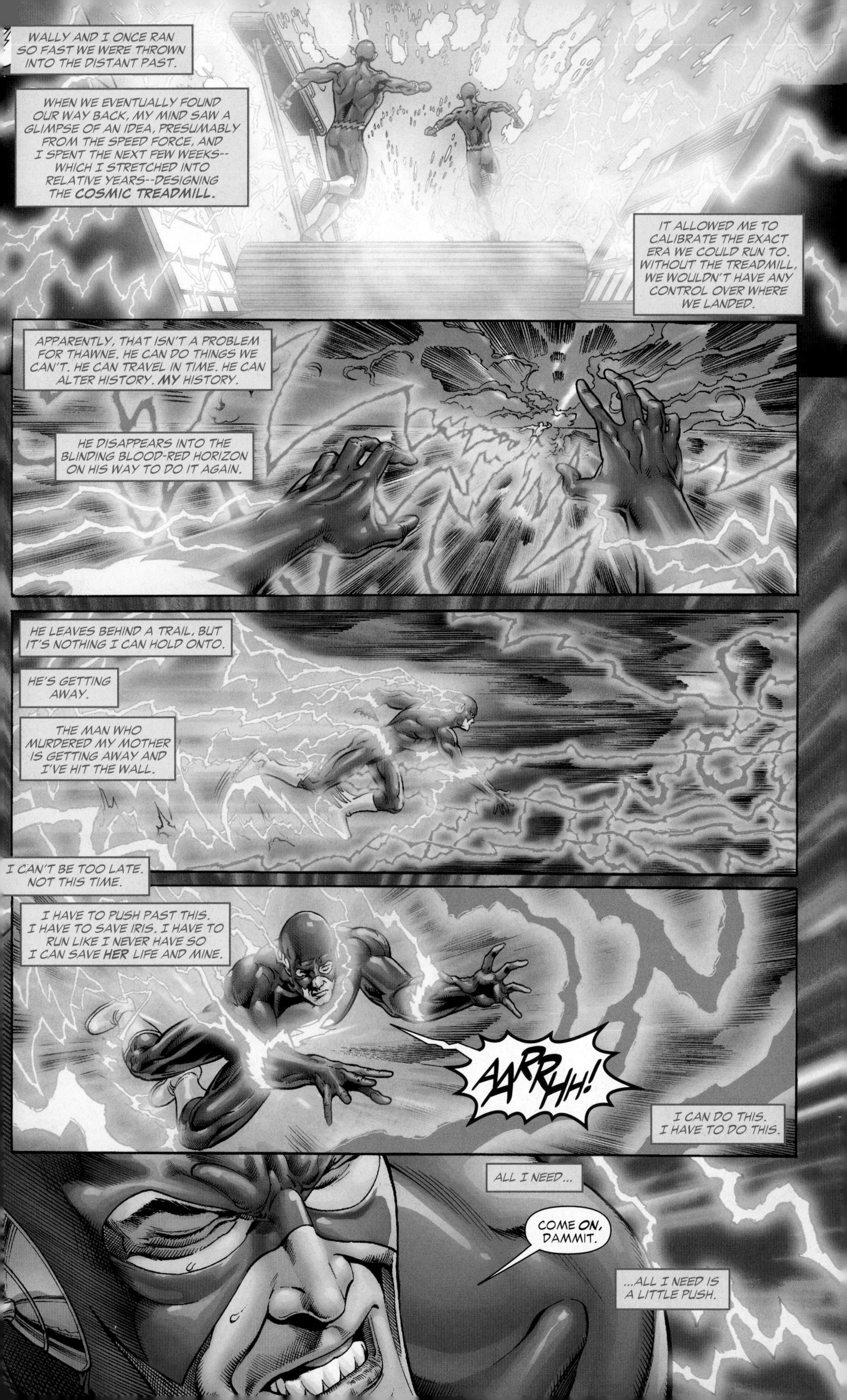

WALLY AND I ONCE RAN SO FAST WE WERE THROWN INTO THE DISTANT PAST.
WHEN WE EVENTUALLY FOUND OUR WAY BACK, MY MIND SAW A GLIMPSE OF AN IDEA, PRESUMABLY FROM THE SPEED FORCE, AND I SPENT THE NEXT FEW WEEKS--WHICH I STRETCHED INTO RELATIVE YEARS--DESIGNING THE COSMIC TREADMILL.
IT ALLOWED ME TO CALIBRATE THE EXACT ERA WE COULD RUN TO. WITHOUT THE TREADMILL, WE WOULDN'T HAVE ANY CONTROL OVER WHERE WE LANDED.
APPARENTLY, THAT ISN'T A PROBLEM FOR THAWNE. HE CAN DO THINGS WE CAN'T. HE CAN TRAVEL IN TIME. HE CAN ALTER HISTORY. MY HISTORY.
HE DISAPPEARS INTO THE BLINDING BLOOD-RED HORIZON ON HIS WAY TO DO IT AGAIN.
HE LEAVES BEHIND A TRAIL, BUT IT'S NOTHING I CAN HOLD ONTO.
HE'S GETTING AWAY.
THE MAN WHO MURDERED MY MOTHER IS GETTING AWAY AND I'VE HIT THE WALL.
I CAN'T BE TOO LATE. NOT THIS TIME.
I HAVE TO PUSH PAST THIS. I HAVE TO SAVE IRIS. I HAVE TO RUN LIKE I NEVER HAVE SO I CAN SAVE HER LIFE AND MINE.
AARRHH!
I CAN DO THIS. I HAVE TO DO THIS.
ALL I NEED...
COME ON, DAMMIT.
...ALL I NEED IS A LITTLE PUSH.

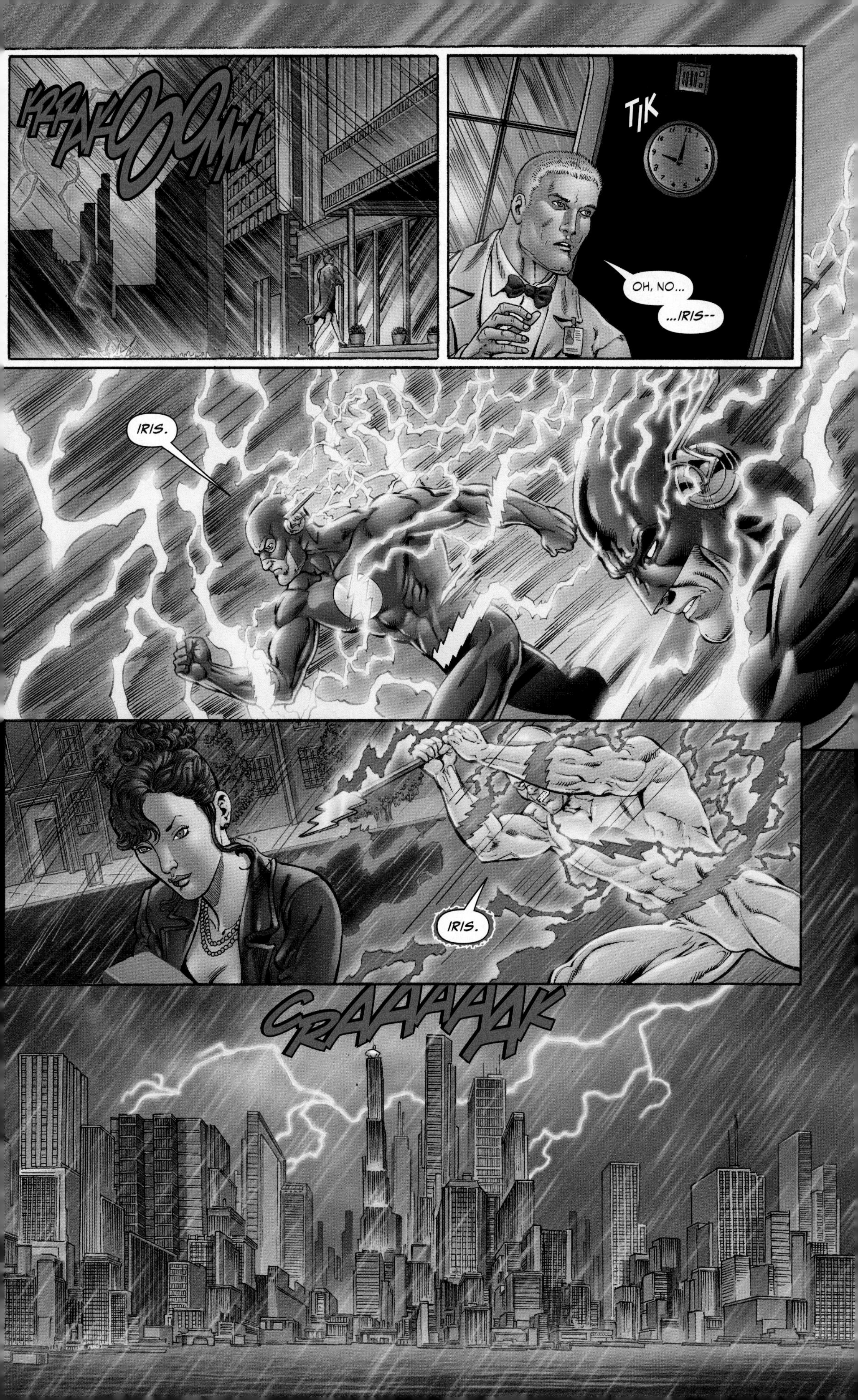
KRRAKOOOMM
TIK
OH, NO...
...IRIS--
IRIS.
IRIS.
GRAAAAAK

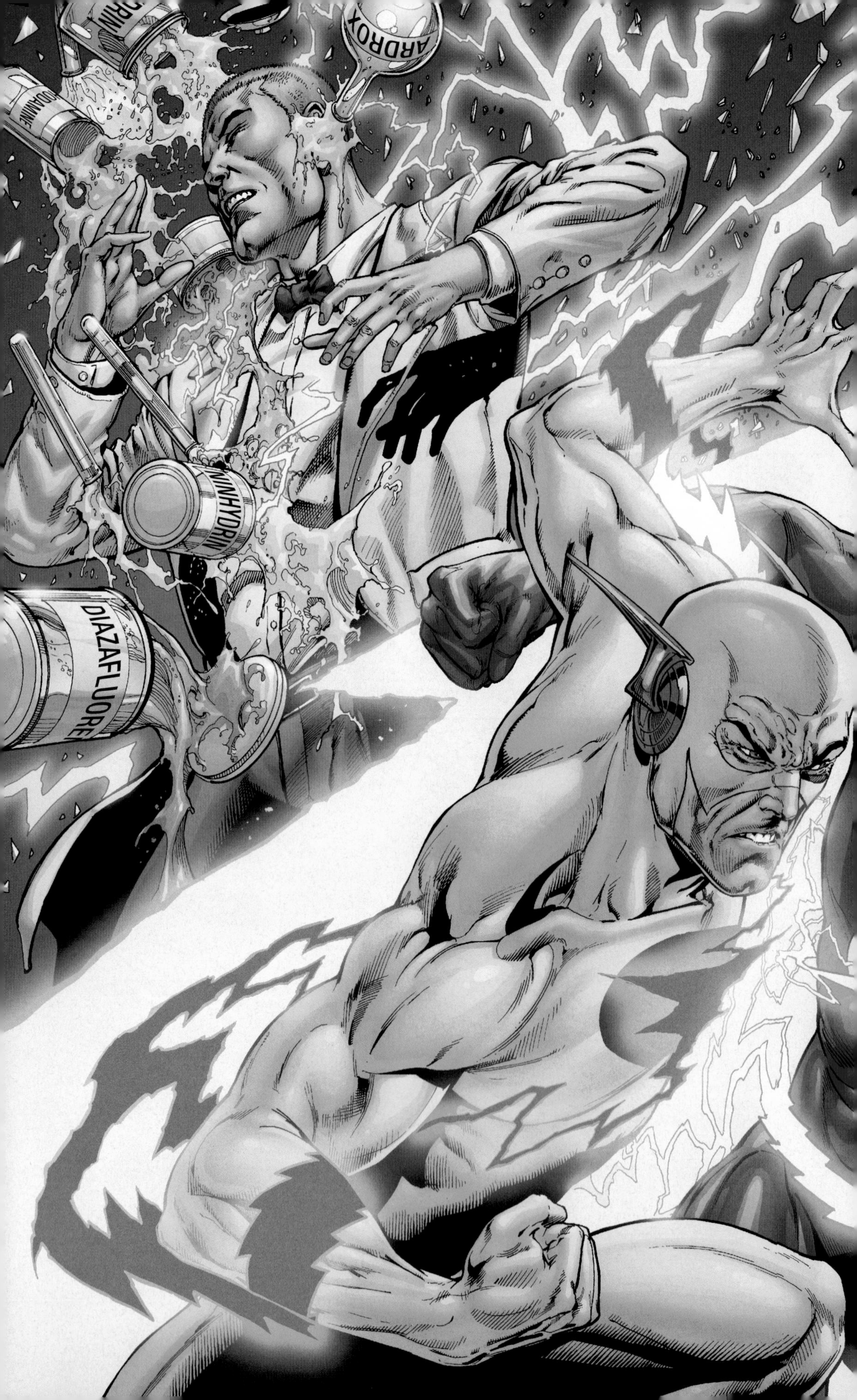
ARDROX
NINHYDRIN
DIAZAFLUORE

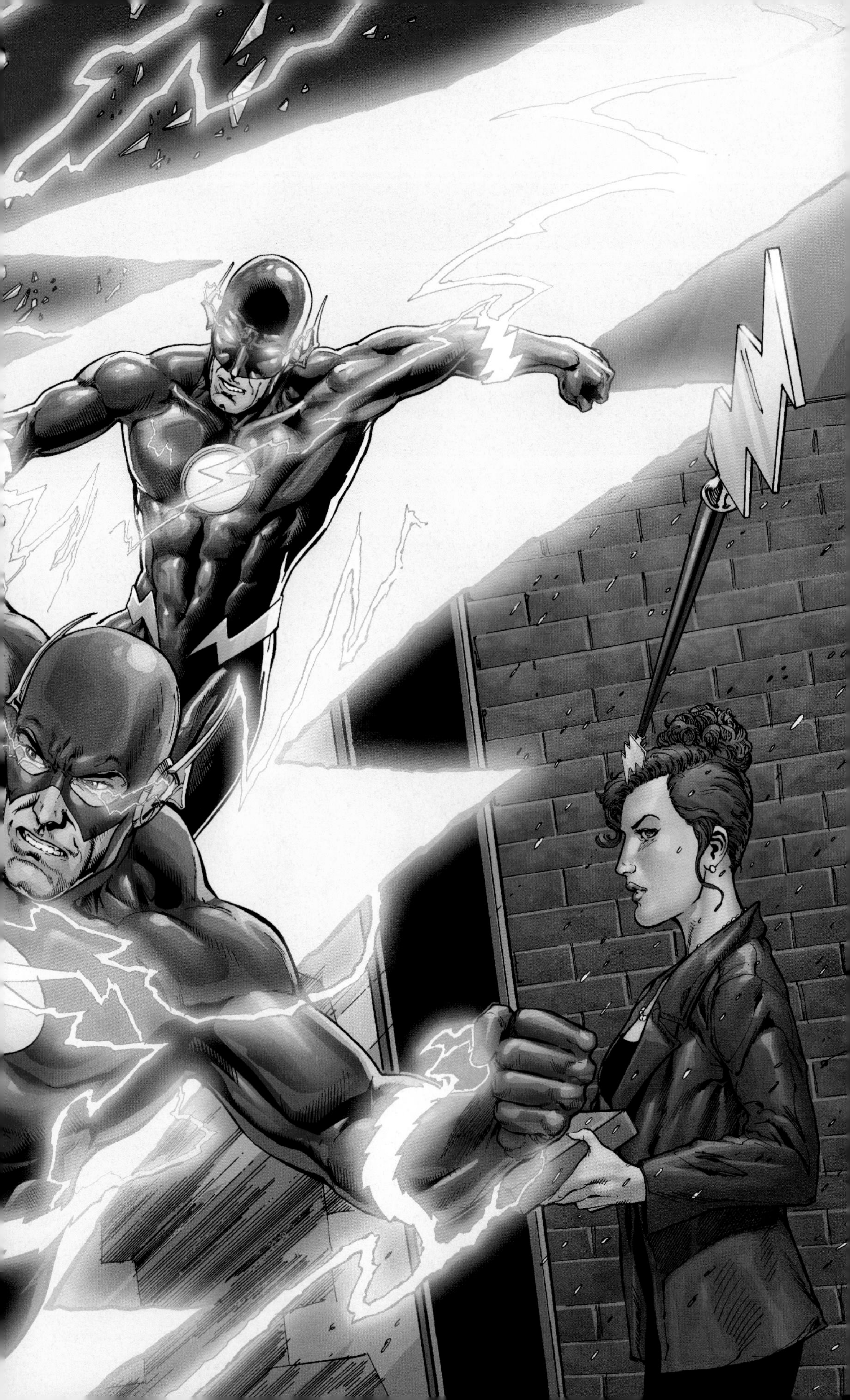

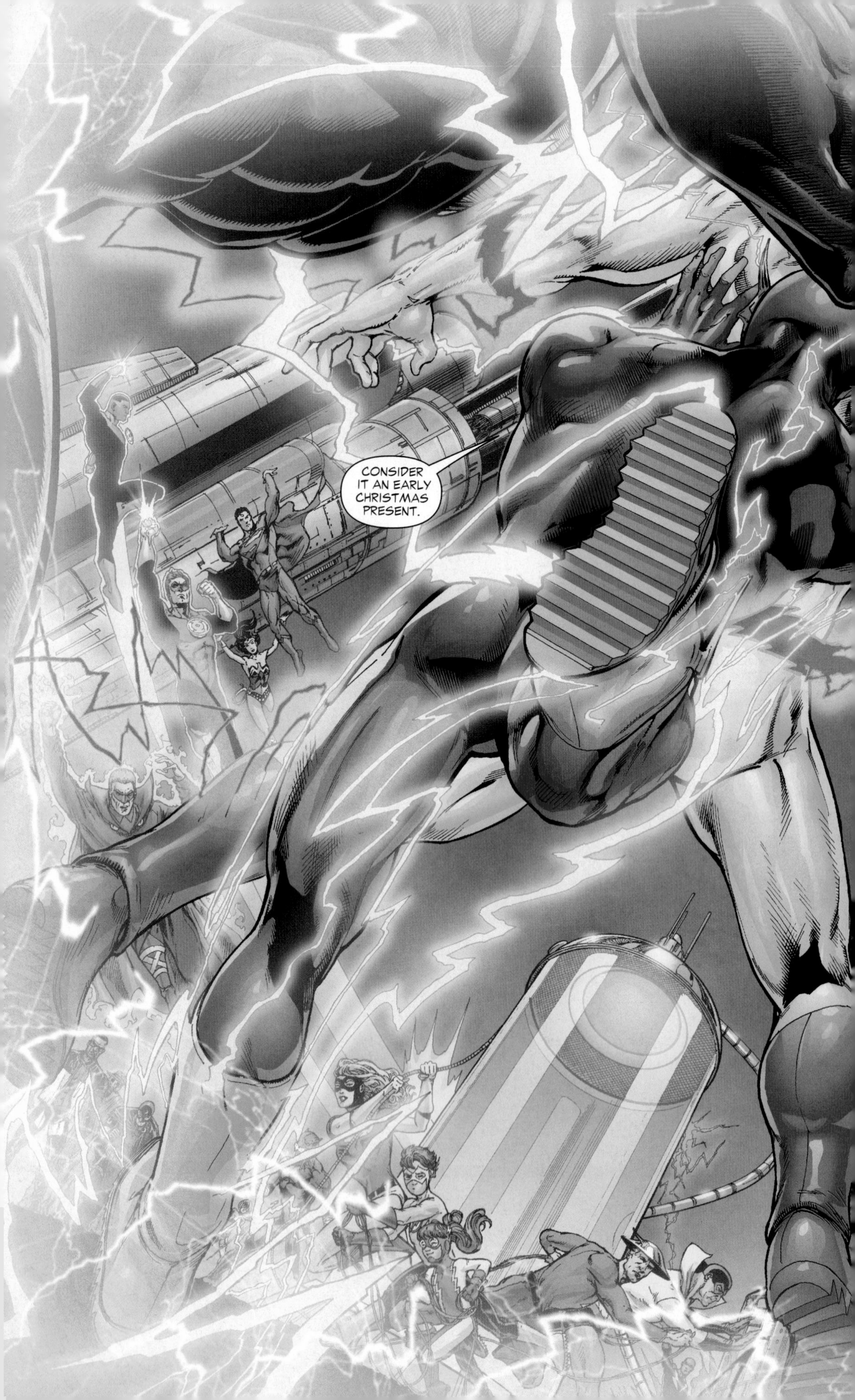
CONSIDER IT AN EARLY CHRISTMAS PRESENT.

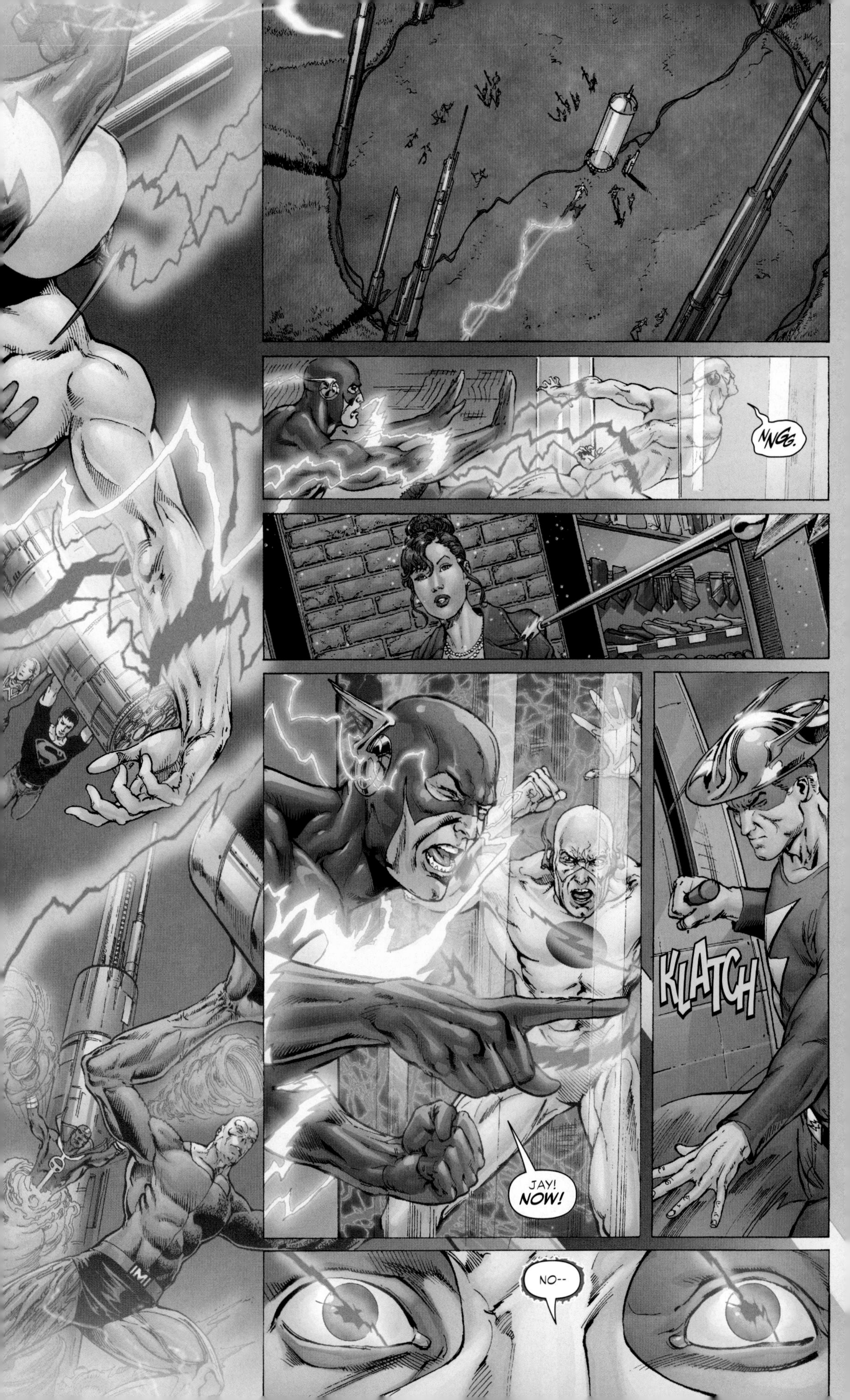
NNGG.
JAY! NOW!
KLATCH
NO--

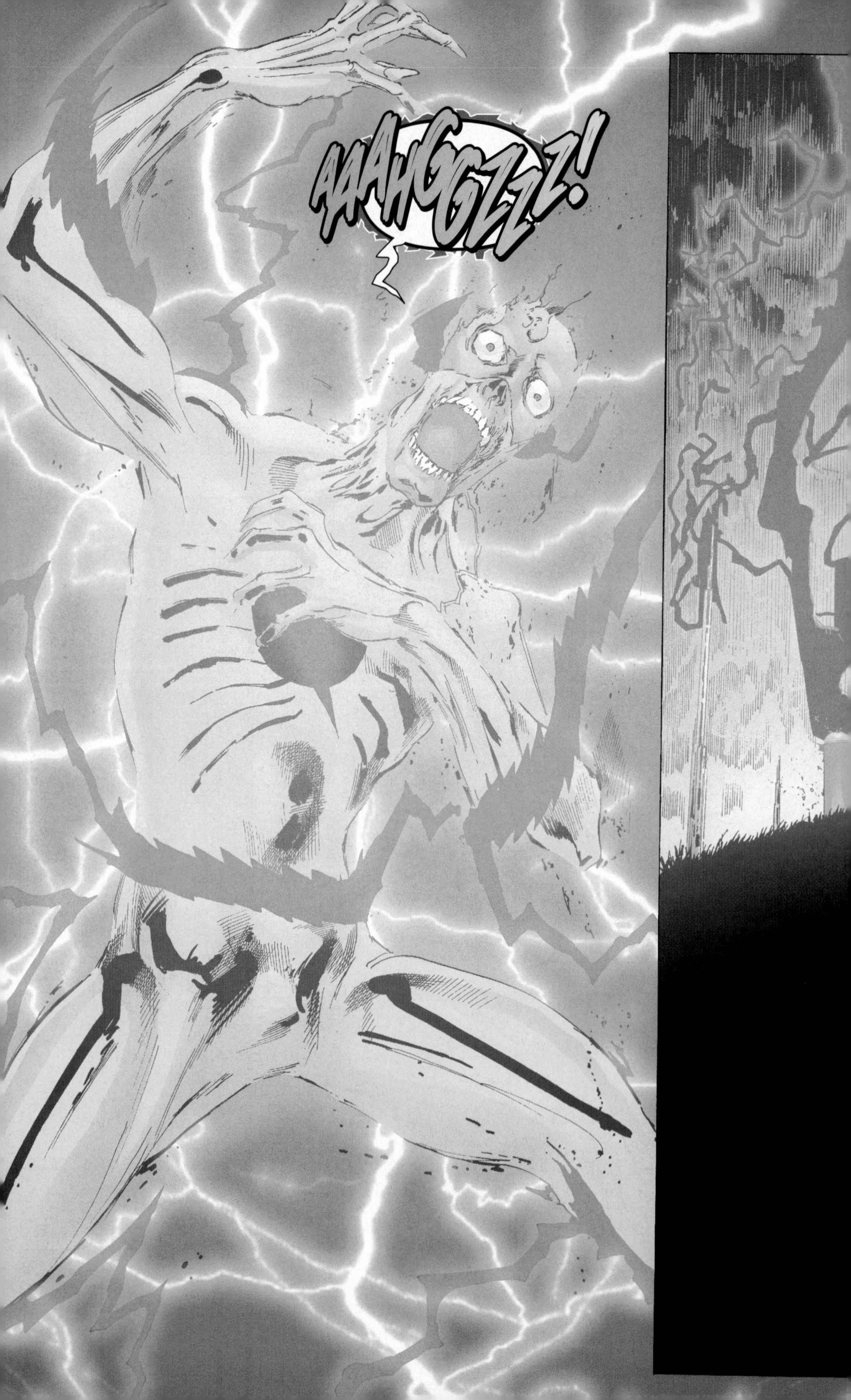
AAAHGGZZZZ!

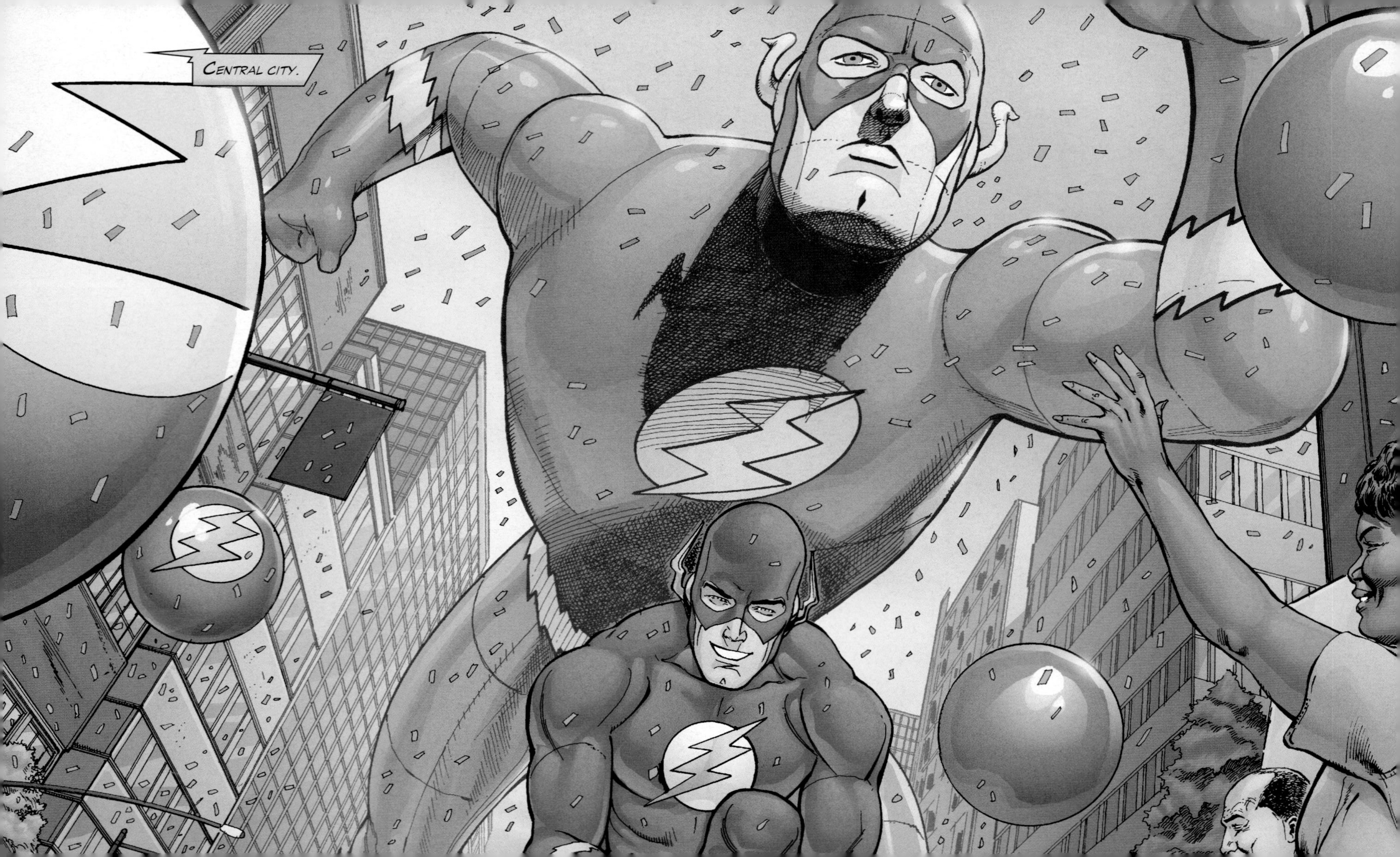
CENTRAL CITY.

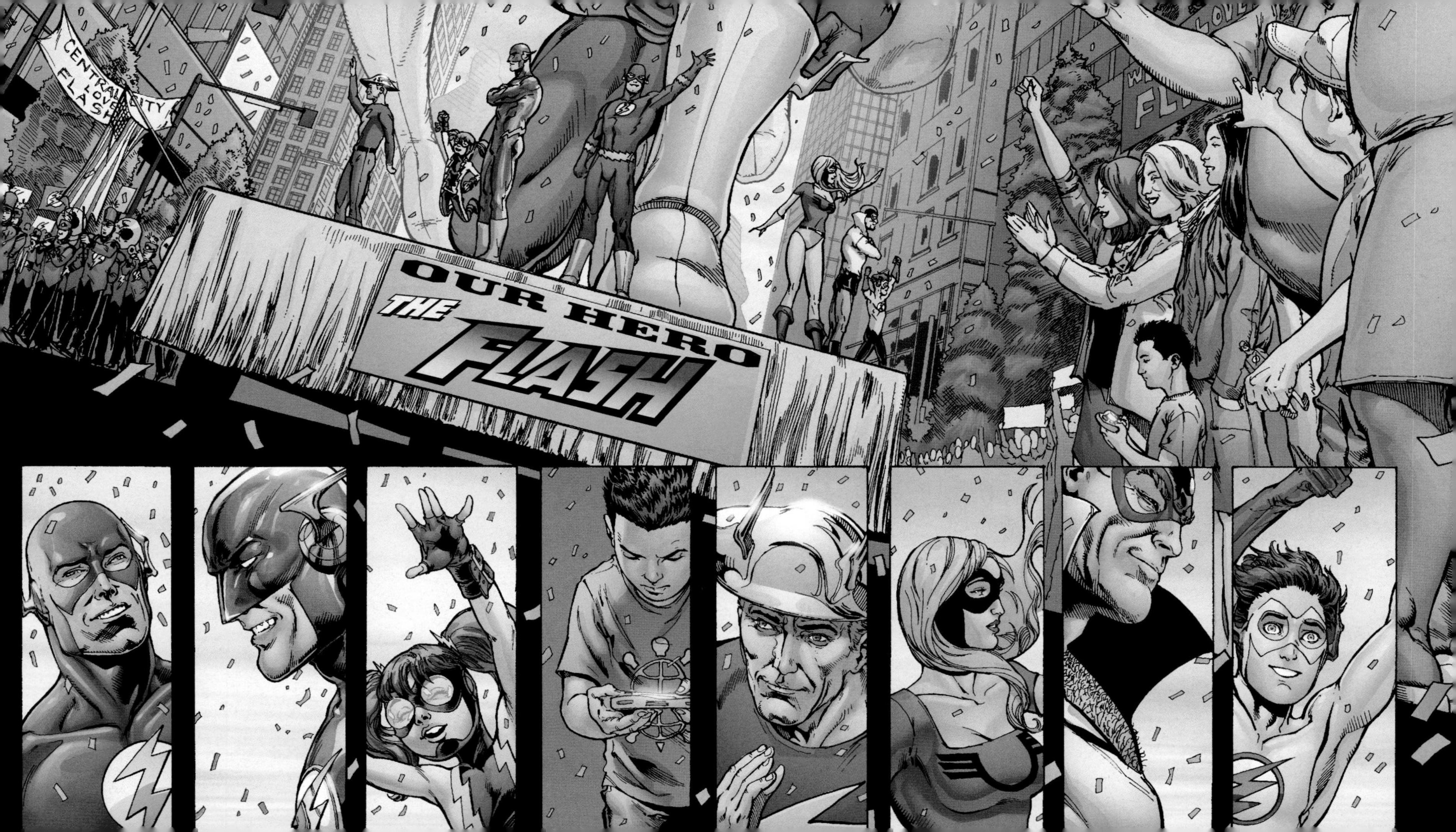
CENTRAL CITY LOVES FLASH
OUR HERO
THE FLASH

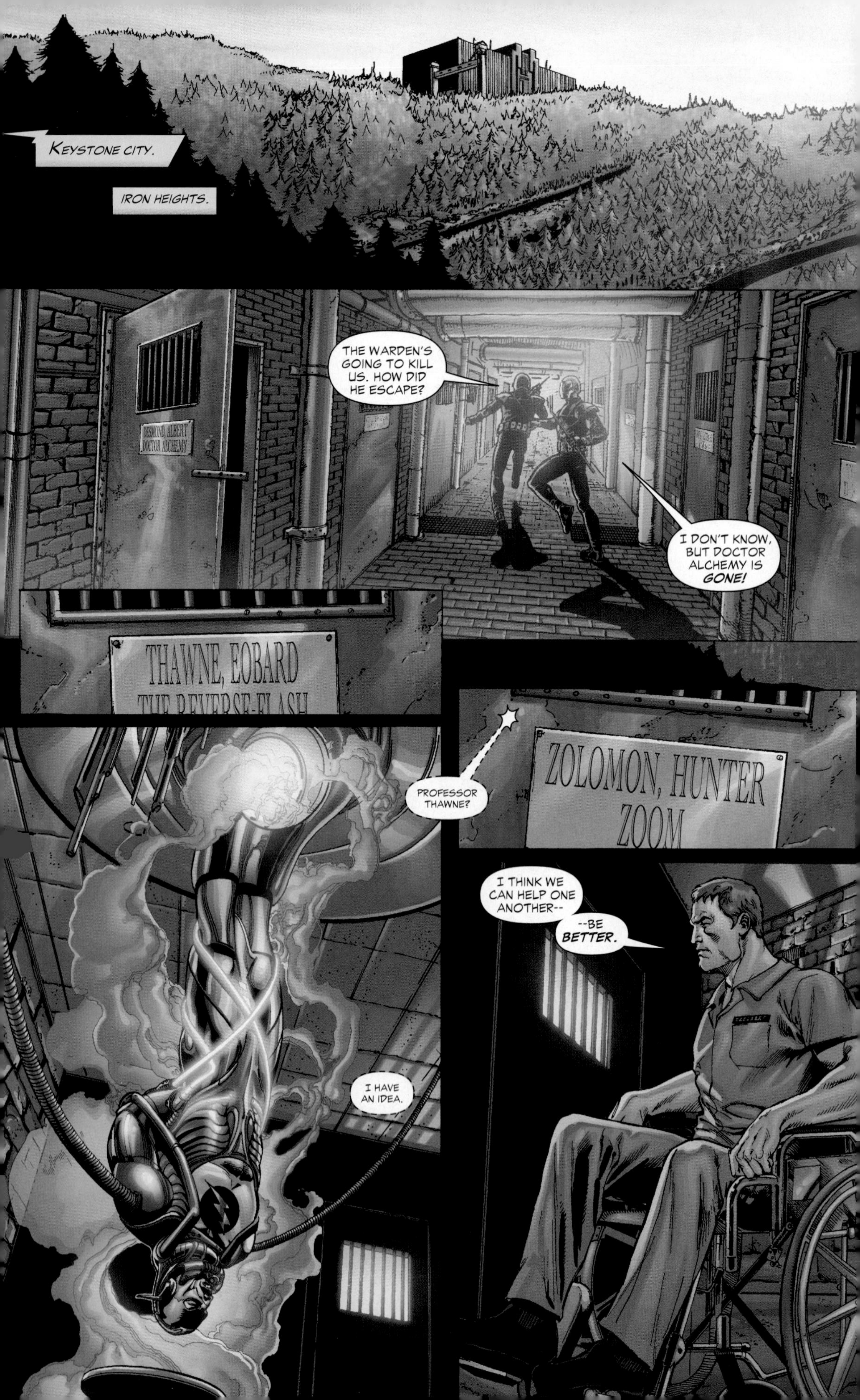
KEYSTONE CITY.
IRON HEIGHTS.
THE WARDEN'S GOING TO KILL US. HOW DID HE ESCAPE?
DESMOND, ALBERT DOCTOR ALCHEMY
I DON'T KNOW, BUT DOCTOR ALCHEMY IS GONE!
THAWNE, EOBARD
ZOLOMON, HUNTER ZOOM
PROFESSOR THAWNE?
I THINK WE CAN HELP ONE ANOTHER--
--BE BETTER.
I HAVE AN IDEA.

THE CONGO BASIN, AFRICA.

GORILLA CITY.

AAH OOO

AAAAAHH!

OOOOOAAH!

AAAAAHH!

MY BROTHERS AND SISTERS, I FEAR IT IS WORSE THAN WE IMAGINED.

HE'S DONE SOMETHING TO OUR JUNGLES.

SOMETHING UNNATURAL.

YOU WANTED TO KEEP ME OUT OF THIS, PROFESSOR--

--YOU SHOULD HAVE MADE SURE I WAS DEAD.

I HAVE MUCH MORE UP MY SLEEVE THAN YOU COULD IMAGINE.

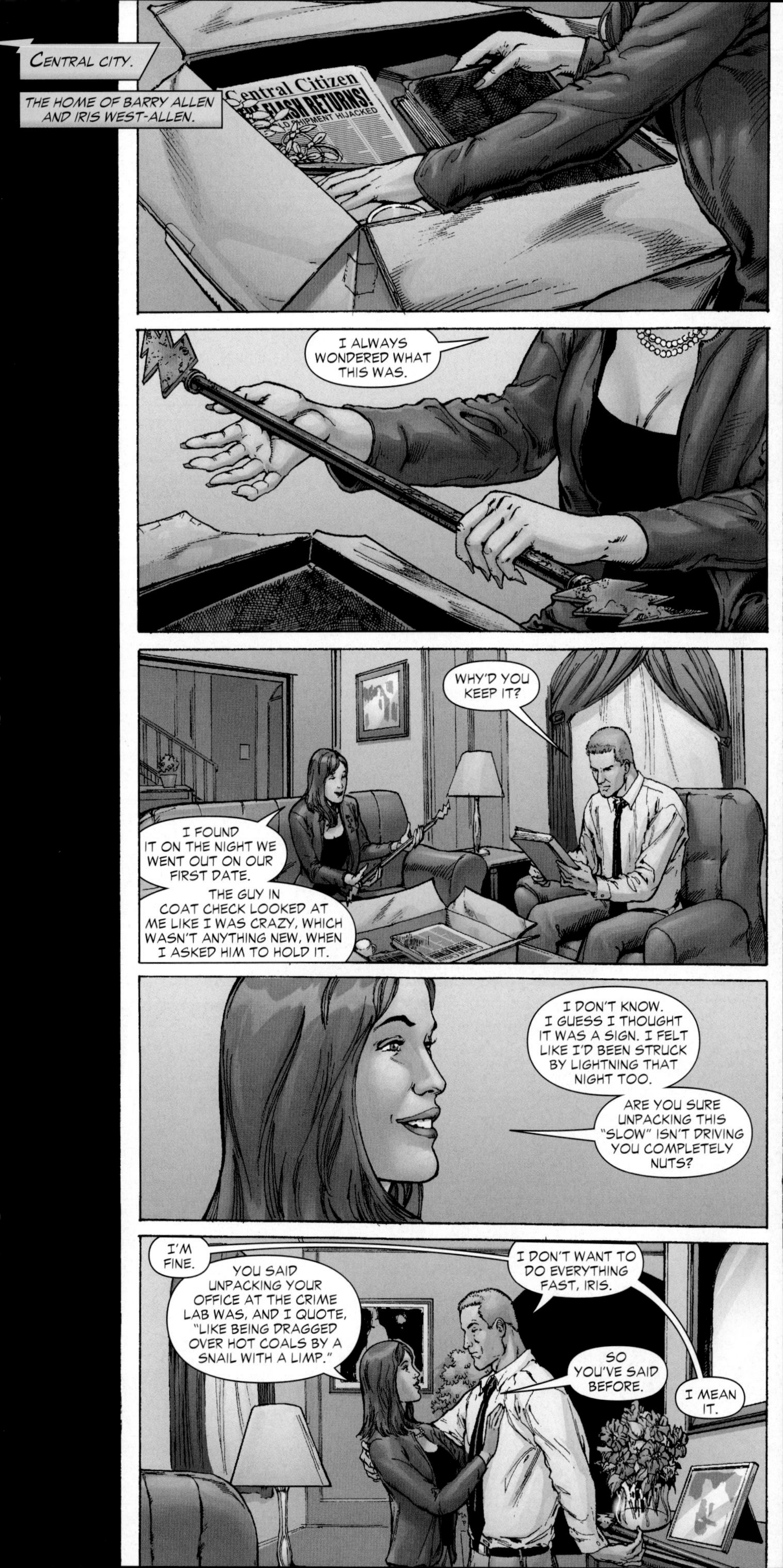
CENTRAL CITY.
THE HOME OF BARRY ALLEN AND IRIS WEST-ALLEN.
Central Citizen
FLASH RETURNS!
I ALWAYS WONDERED WHAT THIS WAS.
WHY'D YOU KEEP IT?
I FOUND IT ON THE NIGHT WE WENT OUT ON OUR FIRST DATE.
THE GUY IN COAT CHECK LOOKED AT ME LIKE I WAS CRAZY, WHICH WASN'T ANYTHING NEW, WHEN I ASKED HIM TO HOLD IT.
I DON'T KNOW. I GUESS I THOUGHT IT WAS A SIGN. I FELT LIKE I'D BEEN STRUCK BY LIGHTNING THAT NIGHT TOO.
ARE YOU SURE UNPACKING THIS "SLOW" ISN'T DRIVING YOU COMPLETELY NUTS?
I'M FINE.
YOU SAID UNPACKING YOUR OFFICE AT THE CRIME LAB WAS, AND I QUOTE, "LIKE BEING DRAGGED OVER HOT COALS BY A SNAIL WITH A LIMP."
I DON'T WANT TO DO EVERYTHING FAST, IRIS.
SO YOU'VE SAID BEFORE.
I MEAN IT.

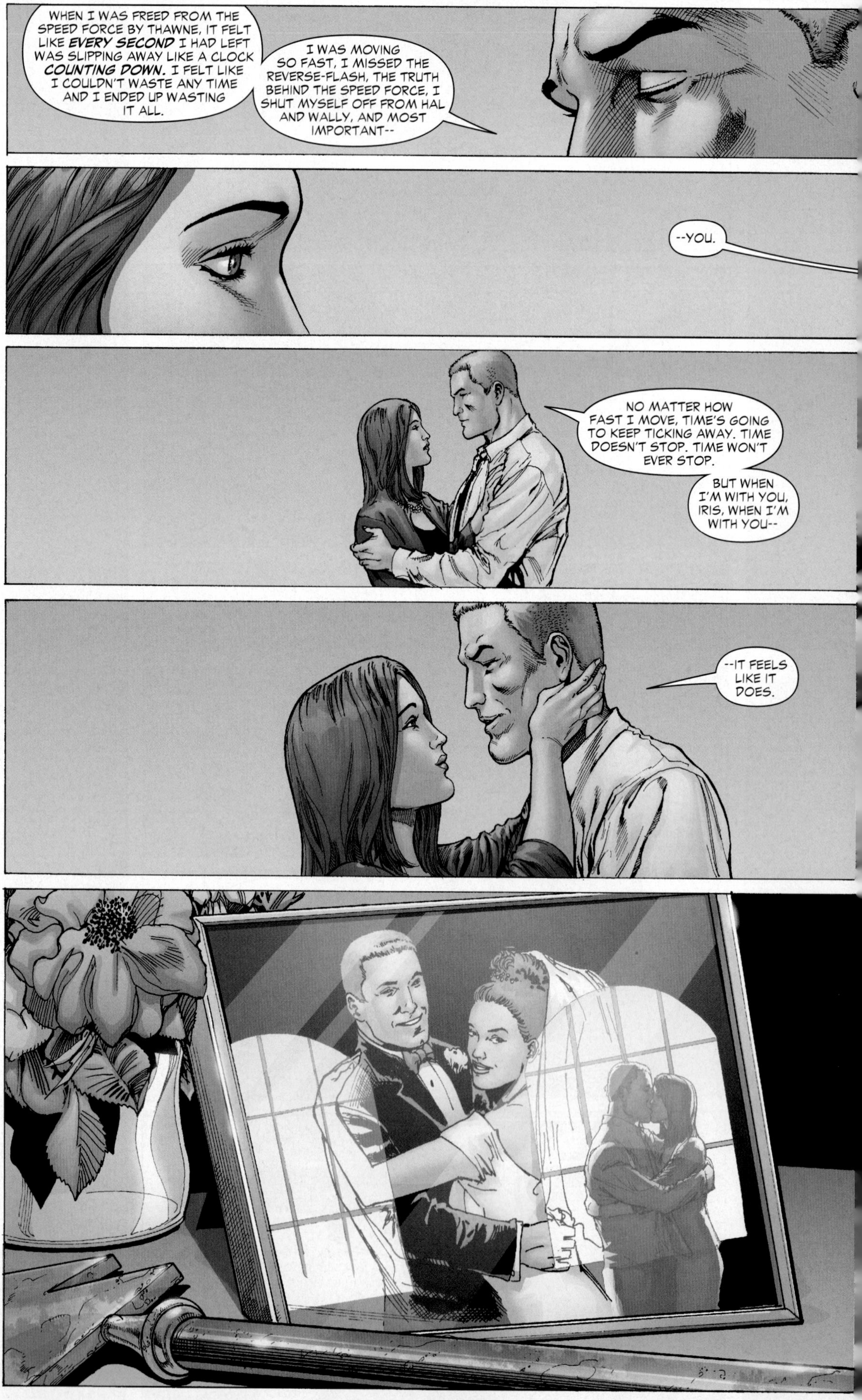
WHEN I WAS FREED FROM THE SPEED FORCE BY THAWNE, IT FELT LIKE **EVERY SECOND** I HAD LEFT WAS SLIPPING AWAY LIKE A CLOCK **COUNTING DOWN.** I FELT LIKE I COULDN'T WASTE ANY TIME AND I ENDED UP WASTING IT ALL.
I WAS MOVING SO FAST, I MISSED THE REVERSE-FLASH, THE TRUTH BEHIND THE SPEED FORCE, I SHUT MYSELF OFF FROM HAL AND WALLY, AND MOST IMPORTANT--
--YOU.
NO MATTER HOW FAST I MOVE, TIME'S GOING TO KEEP TICKING AWAY. TIME DOESN'T STOP. TIME WON'T EVER STOP.
BUT WHEN I'M WITH YOU, IRIS, WHEN I'M WITH YOU--
--IT FEELS LIKE IT DOES.

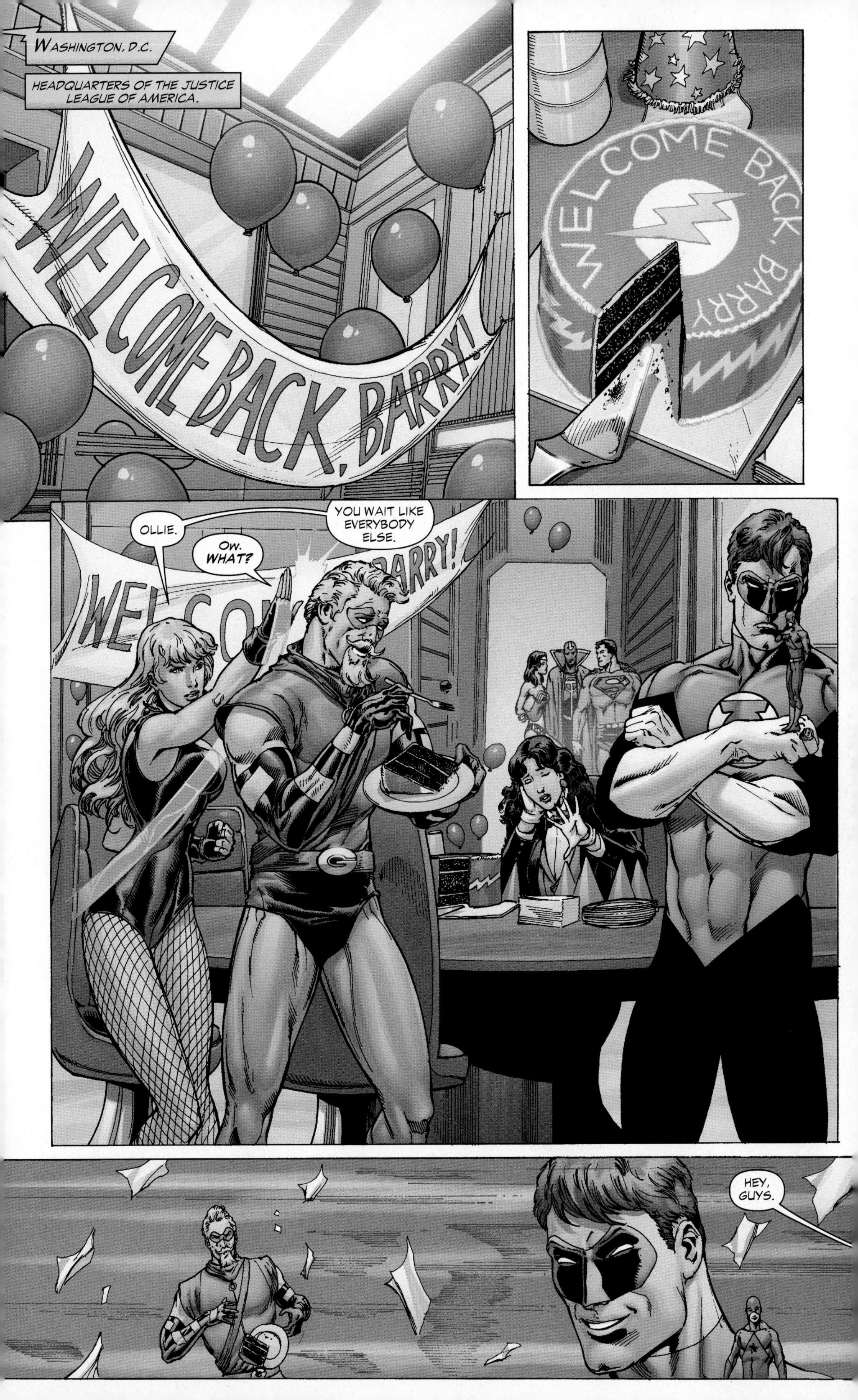
WASHINGTON, D.C.
HEADQUARTERS OF THE JUSTICE LEAGUE OF AMERICA.
WELCOME BACK, BARRY!
WELCOME BACK, BARRY
OLLIE.
OW. WHAT?
YOU WAIT LIKE EVERYBODY ELSE.
HEY, GUYS.

Barry Allen's first appearance in SHOWCASE #4 was the original "rebirth" of the DC Universe. Barry Allen ushered in the Silver Age. His success arguably saved super-heroes.

Springing out of FINAL CRISIS in early 2009, I'd love nothing more than to get a chance to attempt to rebuild Barry Allen and the Flash Universe the same way we've managed to rebuild Hal Jordan and the Green Lantern Universe.

Like the proposal for GREEN LANTERN: REBIRTH, I'm going to outline the basics behind the re-exploration of the Flash mythology. This is about using the best elements and characters from the Flash universe, as we did with Green Lantern, and moving it all forward with Barry Allen front and center.

WHO ARE THE MAIN PLAYERS?

Barry Allen explodes out of the Speed Force during FINAL CRISIS. I hope this proposal illustrates why he should stick around.

The other main characters in this mini-series will include Wally West, Bart Allen (who returns as KID FLASH in 2009), Jay Garrick, Wally's twins, "Iris" West-Allen and Barry's closest friends from the Justice League.

In addition, Max Mercury, the guru of the Speed Force, will return.

WHAT IS THE SECRET OF THE SPEED FORCE?

The Speed Force is a fantastic modern addition to the Flash mythos. But the true origin of the Speed Force has never been revealed. One of the major revelations in THE FLASH: REBIRTH is to reveal that origin:

The night Barry Allen was doused in chemicals and struck by lightning wasn't the night he simply "tapped" into the Speed Force. It was the night Barry Allen created the Speed Force.

The analogy of electricity and positive and negative charges will be a major part of this series. Barry is literally a human electrical generator. His muscles create the electrical energy that adds to the Speed Force. The Speed Force has been tapped and used by Wally, Jay, Bart and a host of other DCU speedsters. Since Barry's "death," the Speed Force hasn't grown.

When Barry returns, that all changes.

WHAT IS BARRY ALLEN'S TRUE LEGACY?

Without Barry Allen the Speed Force would not exist. Without Barry Allen the Flash would not exist.

With the new secret of the Speed Force revealed, Barry Allen's legacy extends well beyond Wally West and Bart Allen. He is the father of thousands of heroes.

The Speed Force that Barry created exists in all of space and time. Meaning, no matter what time period you're in, the Speed Force is there. This explains why, even in the '40s, Jay Garrick was able to tap into the Speed Force.

Again, when Barry Allen first appeared in SHOWCASE #4 in 1956 he ushered in a Silver Age of heroes that was literally a "rebirth" for the DC Universe. Taking what he means within the text of comic book history and applying that to his character you can think of his legacy another way...

When Barry Allen runs he generates more Speed Force. The Speed Force grows. It exists in all of space and time. So as Barry runs and the Speed Force grows, someone else — somewhere and somewhen — is able to tap into the Speed Force and become a great hero.

Although we won't see it, the idea is that Barry Allen is literally expanding his heroic legacy with every step he runs.

WHY SHOULD BARRY ALLEN RETURN AS DC'S MAIN FLASH?

Like Hal Jordan, Barry Allen is an icon. His origin is simple and straightforward. His secret identity as a "police scientist" is as thrilling as his masked identity as the scarlet speedster (and more relevant today than ever). And his personality and relationships within the DC Universe have never been explored in this modern age of comics.

Barry will be the Flash that created the Speed Force.

I believe Barry is as important to the DC Universe as Hal Jordan.

Also, readers can be skeptical about the "big events" in the DC Universe. It's natural and I'm right there with them. But Barry Allen's return truly makes FINAL CRISIS feel like it deserves the title "FINAL." It's the final Crisis for Barry and it's truly CRISIS ON INFINITE EARTHS coming full circle. Although his actual return is already in FINAL CRISIS, it will be explored in THE FLASH: REBIRTH.

WHO IS BARRY ALLEN?

We all had heroes we looked up to when we were children. Sometimes, when we grow up,

we have a chance to meet those heroes. And one of the most crushing things in life is meeting a hero who doesn't live up to your expectations of who you think they really are.

When you meet Barry Allen he surpasses those expectations.

Barry Allen is a valued member of the Central City C.S.I. team, but he's not the leader. Barry loves talking shop. In fact, he'd rather talk shop than anything else.

Barry was known to chat about forensics and technique with Batman for hours after a Justice League meeting ended. Batman never talked to anyone else that long.

Although Barry is much more introverted than Hal, the two are both cops. They have a similar set of morals when it comes to enforcing the law. Despite Barry keeping his feet on the ground and Hal flying off into space, they can relate to the ups and downs of organized law enforcement. No one made Barry laugh quite like Hal, and Hal was one of the few who got Barry's straight-faced humor.

Barry never really liked Green Arrow. He over-heard Ollie talk about the "growing problems of police brutality" one too many times. Barry saw Ollie as the guy who would get his best friend in the League, Hal, in trouble. He made Hal doubt himself on occasion. Barry and Ollie would never be comfortable hanging out together outside the League.

When Hal wanted to go to the bar, Ollie was always his wingmen with the women. Hal would invite Barry along, but Barry would decline. Barry was never good with women.

He married young when he met his soul mate, Iris. And when Iris died, he stumbled through a few relationships.

Barry loves being a cop. He loves piecing together evidence that not only solves the crime, but puts the criminal away. His moral code is unshakable.

Barry's intense when it comes to work, but he also has a dry wit about him. Barry is courageous. He's incorruptible (though he'll find out some of the Central City police are not).

Despite his altered perception, Barry never gets bored. He has incredible patience. Despite his quirks, and there are many, Barry's one of the purest and greatest heroes in the DC Universe.

And, of course, no matter how fast he is, Barry is always, always late.

IF BARRY'S BACK, WHAT HAPPENS TO WALLY WEST?
Like GREEN LANTERN: REBIRTH we aren't here to throw anything away or limit who is on stage, we're here to build it up into a sub-universe like Batman's and Superman's, and now Green Lantern's. Wally is still Wally, yet a Wally West with a second chance at fatherhood. He will do what he has done since day one of FLASH #1: lead and expand the legacy of the Flash with both his children and Flashes from across time, including the return of John Fox.

Wally West's kids have been growing unnaturally thanks to the Speed Force and it could kill them, as established in the current FLASH title. They have not had normal childhoods. When all is said and done, Wally's kids are "cured" and safe, though his daughter is now the new Impulse while his son loses his powers and earns the nickname "the Turtle."

Wally West will work as an auto mechanic for the police department as he has before, therefore allowing him to interact with Barry.

WHAT IS THE NEGATIVE SPEED FORCE?
The opening scene of THE FLASH: REBIRTH would be a silhouetted figure breaking and entering into the Central City Police Lab in the middle of the night. The silhouetted figure puts several deliberately chosen chemicals on a rack by a window.

He waits.

Then lightning hits in a twisted version of Barry Allen's origin!

At this moment, just like Barry created the Speed Force, this silhouetted figure has created the "Negative" Speed Force. Yin and yang — the more this figure runs, the greater the "Negative" Speed Force grows. The greater the "Negative" Speed Force grows, the more it eats away at the Speed Force.

The more this mysterious figure runs, the more he damages the speedsters tapping into the Speed Force. If he runs enough, this villain will destroy the Speed Force, and kill everyone tapping into it.

This mysterious figure will be revealed to be a time-traveling Eobard Thawne — a.k.a. Professor Zoom — a.k.a. Reverse-Flash.

Thawne has discovered the true origin of the Speed Force and has purposely set out to make its opposite charge.

Thawne knows one day Barry will kill him, but he plans to destroy the Flash legacy in revenge for it and put the guilt on Barry himself.

WHAT HAPPENS TO THE OTHER SPEEDSTERS IN THE FLASH: REBIRTH?

After the creation of the "Negative" Speed Force, unbeknownst to Barry it begins to affect the Speed Force.

At first, Jay and Bart and Wally have bursts of super-speed. All over the DC Universe, speedsters' powers are growing and increasing.

Then they do the opposite. Speedsters start to get ill. Some lose their powers.

All but Barry.

Everyone (and the reader) will be led to believe that by the end of this Barry may not only be the last speedster running, but the others will.

That's exactly what Reverse-Flash wants.

As Barry struggles with it (even transforming into the Black Flash) and the Speed Force is eaten away, the other speedsters held in it — Max Mercury, Johnny Quick and Savitar — are expelled. Max Mercury is the one that witnessed the creation and invasion of the "Negative" Speed Force.

But the physical problems Barry has to solve and overcome aren't the only things challenging him...he's also emotionaly distant. Pulled away from everyone.

But he doesn't know why...

WHAT HAS THE REVERSE-FLASH DONE?

One power the Reverse-Flash has that the Flashes have never been able to conquer is traveling through time and actually changing it. Thawne needs Barry to become the Flash and run in order to keep Thawne's pursuit of power intact, but Thawne wants Barry to be miserable.

Although we won't learn it for a while, we discover Thawne has killed Barry's mother.

This all leads to the new series and ████████
████████████████████████████
████████████████████████████
████████████████████████████
████████████████████████████

And that all leads to FLASHPOINT –
the DC Universe 2011 event.

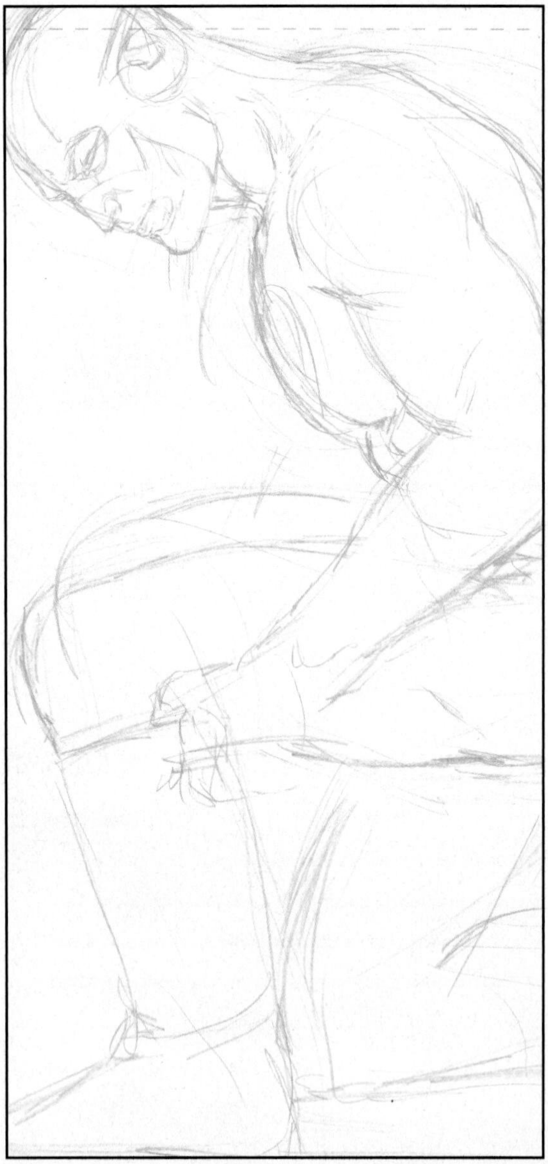

Here's an outtake for the cover of FLASH: REBIRTH #1! Done in blue line pencil, I posed for it myself, just to get the general idea down. From here, I was able to exaggerate the pose to make it more exciting and heroic, and to position the figure to fill almost the entire rectangular frame in a dramatic way.

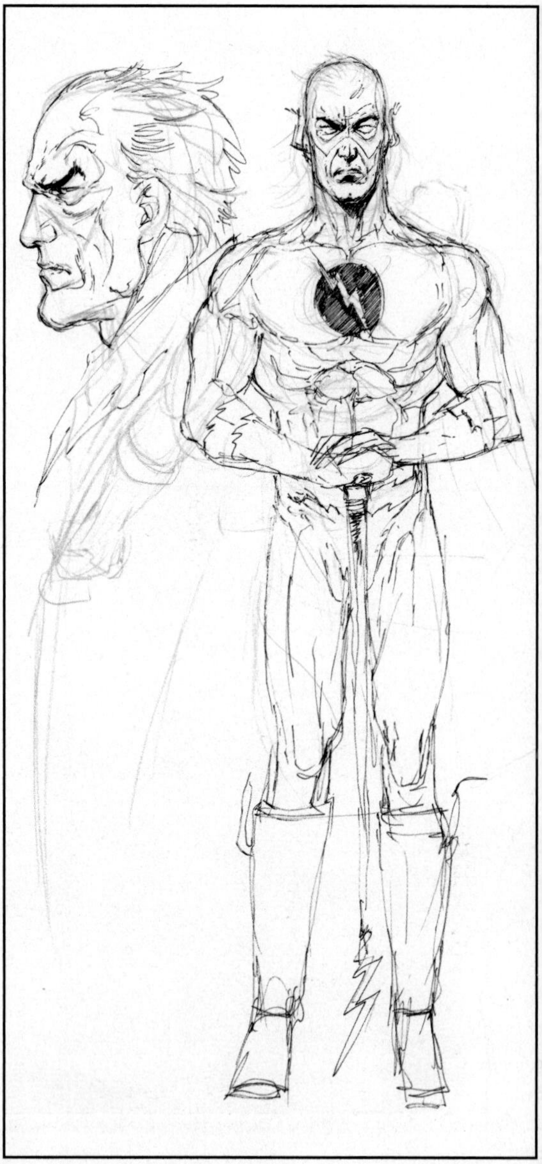

I do so many designs and sketches in airports, when I'm bored. They're never meant to be seen, you see. I do them as a way of thinking. Before we were even sure that Professor Zoom would make his return in FLASH: REBIRTH, I started getting some ideas. Wanting to emphasize the "Professor" part of his name, to make him more scholarly, an academician, I thought he should have some sort of pointing stick, or cane. It became a lightning rod, eventually.

And here it is: I had this drawing of Barry Allen removing his mask done around the same time as the cover to FLASH: REBIRTH #1. I thought I'd turn it into a cover eventually, and decided to take a big chance by DESIGNING WALLY'S COSTUME RIGHT ON THE COVER! Ha ha! That was a daring, and stupid thing to do. But I got very motivated one night, and designed what I thought would be a Guy Gardner- style Flash costume. Big boots, a vest, etc, etc. Nope! I faxed this result to Joey Cavalieri, who asked me if I was out of my mind!

The color version of the Barry image. Used for solicitation of issue #6 only.

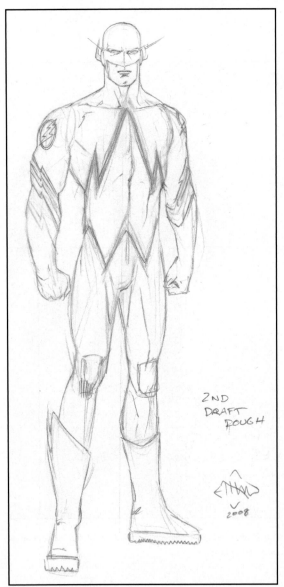

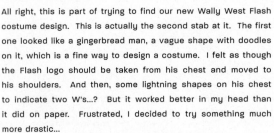

All right, this is part of trying to find our new Wally West Flash costume design. This is actually the second stab at it. The first one looked like a gingerbread man, a vague shape with doodles on it, which is a fine way to design a costume. I felt as though the Flash logo should be taken from his chest and moved to his shoulders. And then, some lightning shapes on his chest to indicate two W's...? But it worked better in my head than it did on paper. Frustrated, I decided to try something much more drastic...

This is obviously an outtake for the FLASH: REBIRTH #2 variant cover. I quit this a few hours into it, because I was becoming aware of how dark and grim I was making our Barry. So lightboxed it and started over.

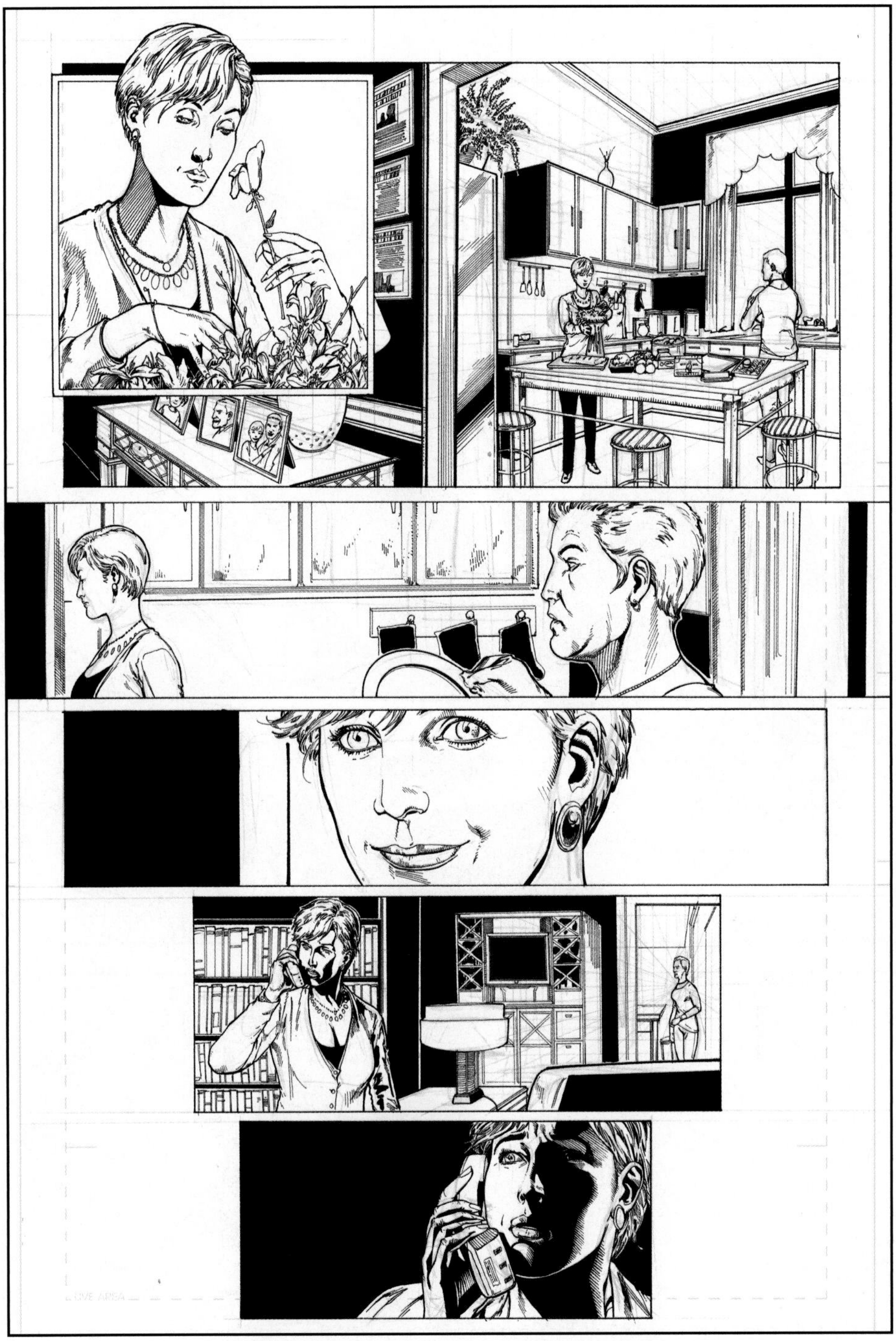

Okay, here's a deleted page from FLASH: REBIRTH #1. And it was deleted and redrawn for good reason. We were never really happy with the quality of the work on the page. This is an older Iris, which I kind of took from what I saw in FINAL CRISIS. Geoff and I knew that one thing that would be revealed about the Speedforce in this miniseries is that it "youthens" the people who come in contact with it. Iris and Barry, as well as Wally, the kids, Bart, Jay would all enjoy a rejuvenation through this story. So I redrew this page with a younger Iris and this page ended up in the circular file.

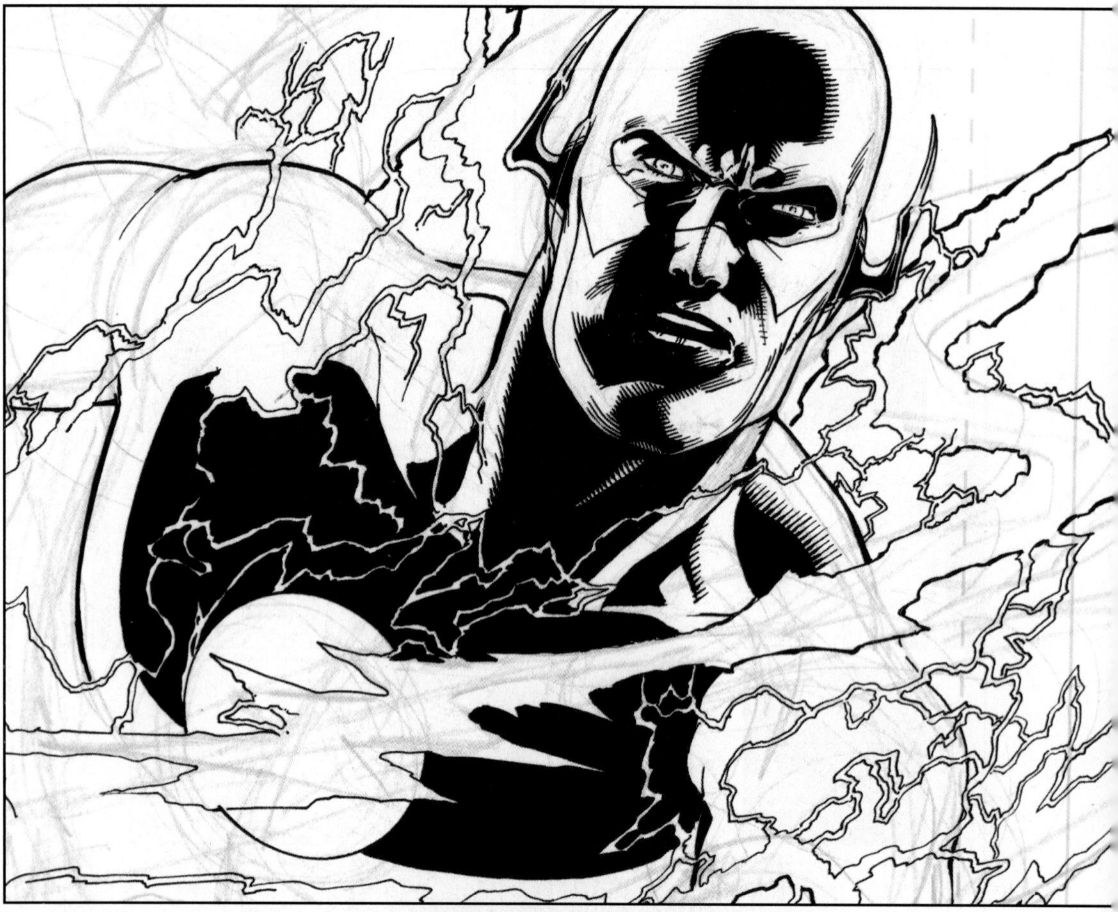

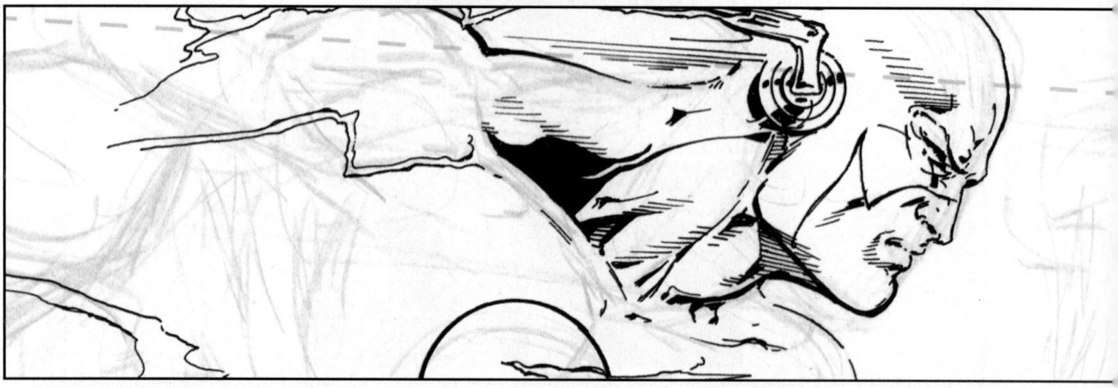

These two sketches probably aren't that interesting. I drew them on an airplane between Newark and Johannesburg, South Africa. Again, I love to draw on planes and in airports, but that doesn't mean that the result is any good! Still, they were done in betwee work on issues #2 and #3, so I include them for the heck of it.

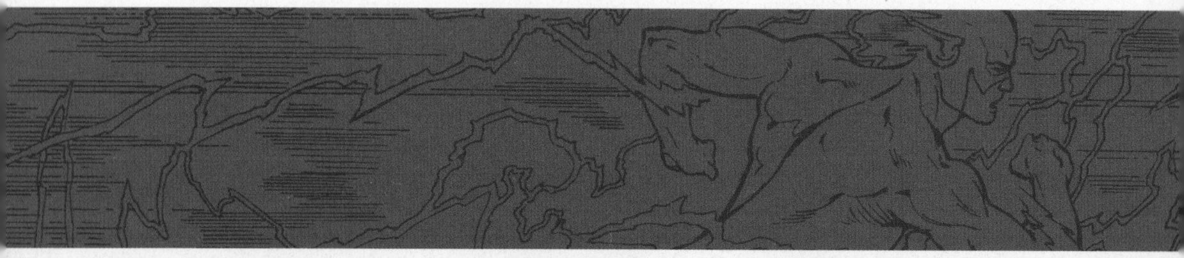